Top Accounting and Auditing Issues for 2021 | CPE Course

Kelen Camehl, CPA
Lynn Fountain, CPA, CGMA, CRMA
Robert K. Minniti, CPA, CFE, CrFA, CVA, CFF, MAFF, CGMA, PI, DBA
Cecil Patterson, Jr., CPA, MBA

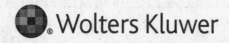

Contributors

Contributing Editor . . . . Kelen Camehl, CPA

Lynn Fountain, CPA, CGMA, CRMA

Robert K. Minniti CPA, CFE, CrFA, CVA, CFF, MAFF, CGMA, PI, DBA

Cecil Patterson, Jr., CPA, MBA

Production Coordinator . . . . Mariela de la Torre; Jennifer Schencker;

Ranjith Rajaram

Production . . . . Sharon Sofinski; Anbarasu Anbumani

This publication is designed to provide accurate and authoritative information in regard to the subject matter covered. It is sold with the understanding that the publisher is not engaged in rendering legal, accounting, or other professional service. If legal advice or other expert assistance is required, the services of a competent professional person should be sought. All views expressed in this publication are those of the author and not necessarily those of the publisher or any other person.

SUSTAINABLE FORESTRY INITIATIVE

Certified Sourcing

www.sfiprogram.org
SFI-01681

ISBN: 978-0-8080-5534-1

© 2020 CCH Incorporated and its affiliates. All rights reserved.
2700 Lake Cook Road
Riverwoods, IL 60015
800 344 3734
CCHCPELink.com

No claim is made to original government works; however, within this Publication, the following are subject to CCH Incorporated's copyright: (1) the gathering, compilation, and arrangement of such government materials; (2) the magnetic translation and digital conversion of data, if applicable; (3) the historical, statutory and other notes and references; and (4) the commentary and other materials.

Do not send returns to the above address. If for any reason you are not satisfied with your book purchase, it can easily be returned within 30 days of shipment. Please go to *support.cch.com/returns* to initiate your return. If you require further assistance with your return, please call: (800) 344-3734 M-F, 8 a.m. – 6 p.m. CT.

Printed in the United States of America

Introduction

Top Accounting and Auditing Issues for 2021 CPE Course helps CPAs stay abreast of the most significant new accounting and auditing standards and important projects. It does so by identifying the events of the past year that have developed into hot issues and reviewing the opportunities and pitfalls presented by these changes. The topics reviewed in this course were selected because of their impact on financial reporting and because of the role they play in understanding the accounting and auditing landscape in the year ahead.

Module 1 of this course reviews top accounting issues.

Chapter 1 provides an overview of post-implementation issues and lessons learned from the new lease standard (ASC 842) and the new credit losses standard (ASC 326).

Chapter 2 outlines the five step revenue recognition model and relevant application for proper compliance with Accounting Standards Update No. 2014-09, *Revenue from Contracts with Customers (Topic 606)*. Although on the surface these steps seem simplistic, there are many considerations to be applied within each step. Considerations can be related to an entities specific processes, industry characteristics as well as contract characteristics.

Module 2 of this course reviews top auditing issues.

Chapter 3 provides a brief review of the background to the changes in auditing standards and then outlines specific changes to Generally Accepted Auditing Standards (GAAS) from the following Statements on Auditing Standards (SAS) released by the AICPA Auditing Standards Board (ASB): SAS No. 134, *Auditor Reporting and Amendments, Including Amendments Addressing Disclosures in the Audit of Financial Statements*; SAS No. 135, *Omnibus Statement on Auditing Standards—2019*; SAS No. 136, *Forming an Opinion and Reporting on Financial Statements of Employee Benefit Plans Subject to ERISA*; SAS No. 137, *The Auditor's Responsibilities Relating to Other Information Included in Annual Reports*; SAS No. 138, *Amendments to the Description of the Concept of Materiality*, and SSAE No. 20 of the same title; SAS No. 139, *Amendments to AU-C Sections 800, 805, and 810 to Incorporate Auditor Reporting Changes from SAS No. 134*; SAS No. 140, *Amendments to AU-C Sections 725, 730, 930, 935, and 940 to Incorporate Auditor Reporting Changes from SAS Nos. 134 and 137*; and SAS No. 141, *Amendment to the Effective Dates of SAS Nos. 134-140*. The chapter also reviews illustrations of audit reports with new changes and updates on other important issues.

Chapter 4 discusses the new standards from the Auditing Standards Board (ASB) that amend the description of the concept of materiality. It provides an overview of Statement on Auditing Standards (SAS) No. 138, *Amendments to the Description of the Concept of Materiality*; Statement on Standards for Attestation Engagements (SSAE) No. 20 (of the same title); and Statements on Standards for Accounting and Review Services (SSARS) 25, *Materiality in a Review of Financial Statements and Adverse Conclusions*. This chapter also discusses SAS No. 141, *Amendments to the Effective Dates of SASs Nos. 134-140*. SAS No. 141 changes the effective dates of SASs Nos. 134-140 from periods ending on or after December 15, 2020, for one year to periods ending on or after December 15, 2021. This was done in order to provide more time to implement SASs Nos. 134-140 due to the COVID-19 pandemic.

Chapter 5 provides an overview of important concepts and updates related to management discussion and analysis (MD&A) as outlined in Topic 9 of the Financial Reporting Manual.

Chapter 6 explains how auditors can use data analytics in an audit. Topics discussed include common uses of data analytics, data formats, types of data analysis, analytical procedures, and Benford's Law.

Module 3 of this course reviews top fraud issues.

Chapter 7 is designed for individuals who would like to refresh their understanding of fraud schemes and to learn how to recognize the red flags for detecting fraud. Understanding how criminals commit fraud is the first step in preventing fraud.

Study Questions. Throughout the course you will find Study Questions to help you test your knowledge, and comments that are vital to understanding a particular strategy or idea. Answers to the Study Questions with feedback on both correct and incorrect responses are provided in a special section beginning at ¶ 10,100.

Final Exam. This course is divided into three Modules. Take your time and review all course Modules. When you feel confident that you thoroughly understand the material, turn to the Final Exam. Complete one or all three Final Exams for continuing professional education credit.

Go to **cchcpelink.com/printcpe** to complete your Final Exam online for immediate results. My Dashboard provides convenient storage for your CPE course Certificates. Further information is provided in the CPE Final Exam instructions at ¶ 10,300. **Please note, manual grading is no longer available for Top Accounting and Auditing Issues. All answer sheets must be submitted online for grading and processing.**

August 2020

PLEDGE TO QUALITY

Thank you for choosing this CCH® CPELink product. We will continue to produce high quality products that challenge your intellect and give you the best option for your Continuing Education requirements. Should you have a concern about this or any other Wolters Kluwer product, please call our Customer Service Department at 1-800-344-3734.

COURSE OBJECTIVES

This course provides an overview of important accounting and auditing developments. At the completion of this course, the reader will be able to:

- Identify the overall requirements related to the new lease standard
- Recognize key lessons learned related to implementation of the new lease standard
- Identify key requirements and guidance related to the new credit losses standard
- Recognize best practices for implementation of the new credit losses standard
- Understand impacts to both standards as a result of the COVID-19 pandemic
- Identify effective dates for the updated revenue recognition standard
- Explain the need for the updated revenue recognition standard
- Recognize and apply the updated revenue recognition core principles and the five-step revenue recognition model
- Identify the impact of the updated revenue recognition standard on various revenue concepts
- Describe the impact of the revenue recognition standard on various industries
- Identify how to implement the new and extensive audit report format, disclosures, and procedures

- Differentiate AU-C sections and how they apply to the auditor's responsibilities

- Recognize when the updates to Statements on Auditing Standards (SAS) sections by the Accounting Standards Board (ASB) are effective

- Identify how AU-C sections apply to financial statements

- Differentiate the "Opinion" section of the auditor's report and what is included

- Identify where the auditor's report should name the city and state

- Describe what should be exercised and maintained by the auditor in accordance with GAAS

- Recognize and apply the concept of materiality to financial applications

- Differentiate the nuances in the definition of materiality

- Recognize and apply the concept of materiality to audit considerations in an audit

- Understand materiality and risks

- Understand the use of materiality in attestation engagements

- Understand the effective date changes of SASs 134-140

- Identify the purpose and objectives of Management Discussion and Analysis (MD&A)

- Understand the typical components included in MD&A

- Identify the updated objective of MD&A disclosures

- Examine details of final amendments

- Examine criteria related to key performance indicators

- Identify various types of data analytics that can be used in an audit

- Recognize how to use Benford's Law in an analysis of data in an audit situation

- Understand theories as to why people commit fraud

- Recognize fraud schemes that affect businesses and individuals

- Identify red flags for fraud

- Recognize the different types of fraud, including occupational fraud, cyber fraud, financial fraud, tax fraud, and identity theft

---

Additional copies of this course may be downloaded from **cchcpelink.com/printcpe**. Printed copies of the course are available for $4.50 by calling 1-800-344-3734 (ask for product 10024493-0008).

Contents

MODULE 1: TOP ACCOUNTING ISSUES— CHAPTER 1: Leases and Credit Losses: Post-implementation and Lessons Learned

¶ 101 WELCOME

This course provides an overview of post-implementation issues and lessons learned from the new lease standard (ASC 842) and the new credit losses standard (ASC 326). The new lease standard was effective for calendar-year public business entities in the first quarter of 2019, whereas the new credit losses standard is effective one year later in January 2020. Each of these standards, since their respective initial release dates, has been subject to additional clarifying accounting standard updates as well as additional guidance provided by various standard setters and other impacted stakeholders.

¶ 102 LEARNING OBJECTIVES

Upon completion of this chapter, you will be able to:

- Identify the overall requirements related to the new lease standard
- Recognize key lessons learned related to implementation of the new lease standard
- Identify key requirements and guidance related to the new credit losses standard
- Recognize best practices for implementation of the new credit losses standard
- Understand impacts to both standards as a result of the COVID-19 pandemic

¶ 103 INTRODUCTION

The first part of this chapter addresses post-implementation issues and lessons learned with respect to the new lease standard, ASC 842. The Financial Accounting Standards Board (FASB) included the new lease accounting guidance within a new ASC 842 instead of modifying the current lease accounting standards within ASC 840. The new lease standard affects nearly all companies and other organizations that lease assets such as ships, airplanes, construction equipment, and real estate.

To establish a good grounding for discussing the relevant lessons learned from the new standard, we'll first provide a background of development of the new standard and the key amendments and changes brought about by the standard.

¶ 104 OVERVIEW OF THE NEW LEASE STANDARD

Nearly 10 years ago in 2006, the FASB and the International Accounting Standards Board (IASB) commenced a joint project to improve the financial reporting of lease activities. Nearly 10 years later, on February 25, 2016, the FASB released the final revised accounting standards with respect to leasing activities through the issuance of FASB Accounting Standards Update (ASU) No. 2016-02, *Leases*. This was only shortly after the IASB released its final version of IFRS 16, *Leases*, on January 13, 2016.

Prior to ASC 842, the existing lease accounting standards did not require that lessees recognize assets and liabilities that arise from operating leases on their balance sheet (i.e., they were "off–balance sheet"). However, recognition on the balance sheet was required as it related to capital leases. The FASB concluded that based on this disconnect between the different accounting models, coupled with the fact that it is common to structure lease transactions to avoid balance sheet recognition, the previous accounting model did not meet the needs of users of financial statements. As a result, the previous lease accounting standards resulted in two significantly different accounting models. One model relates to a situation where a lessee appropriately reflects an asset and liability resulting from a lease transaction. The other model results in favorable, off–balance sheet recognition.

¶ 105 APPLYING THE NEW LEASE STANDARD

The first step in applying the new lease standard is to determine if a contract contains a lease. The determination of whether an arrangement contains a lease or a service agreement is critical because there are differences in accounting for each type of arrangement. By definition, a lease is " . . . a contract, or part of a contract, that conveys the right to control the use of identified property, plant, or equipment (an identified asset) for a period of time in exchange for consideration." A service agreement (i.e., an arrangement that does not contain a lease) is one that is recognized ratably over time under the accrual method of accounting.

The FASB notes within its Basis for Conclusions that in most cases, the assessment of whether a contract contains a lease should be straightforward. To this end, a contract either will fail to meet the definition of a lease by failing to meet many of the requirements or will clearly meet the requirements to be a lease without requiring a significant amount of judgment.

The determination of whether an arrangement contains a lease requires that companies first determine whether there is an identified asset in the contract. Once it is determined that an identified asset exists with respect to the arrangement, the following issues are further considered:

- Does the customer have the right to obtain substantially all of the economic benefits from this identified asset?
- Does the customer have the ability to direct how and for what purpose the identified asset is used throughout the period of use?
- Does the customer have the right to operate the identified asset without supplier intervention?
- Did the customer design the asset or significantly customize it?

A comprehensive discussion of the above factors and the related guidance that impacts the determination of whether an arrangement contains a lease is outside the scope of this chapter. There is extensive guidance included within ASC 842, as well as significant implementation guidance that applies this respective guidance. However, note that depending on an assessment of these factors, it may or may not result in a conclusion that the arrangement contains a lease.

¶ 106 LEASE CLASSIFICATION

Once it has been determined that an arrangement contains a lease, the next step is to conclude on the lease classification. The previous lease accounting standards prescribed the use of two different recognition models for a lessee—the operating lease and the capital lease. While the new standard preserves two different types of leases, the former capital lease is now referred to as a *finance lease*. Under the new guidance, a lessee is required to classify a lease as a finance lease when it meets any one of the following criteria:

- The lease transfers ownership of the underlying asset to the lessee by the end of the lease term.

- The lease grants the lessee an option to purchase the underlying asset that the lessee is reasonably certain to exercise.

- The lease term is for the major part of the remaining economic life of the underlying asset.

- The present value of the sum of the lease payments and any residual value guaranteed by the lessee that is not already reflected in the lease payments equals or exceeds substantially all of the fair value of the underlying asset.

- The underlying asset is of such a specialized nature that it is expected to have no alternative use to the lessor at the end of the lease term.

Generally, the criteria used to distinguish between the two types of leases remains fairly unchanged in principle; however, the bright lines (e.g., 75 percent or more of the economic life and 90 percent used in the minimum lease payments) have been removed from the guidance. Instead, the criteria have been replaced with more judgmental terms such as "major part of the remaining economic life" and "substantially all of the fair value of the underlying asset." However, in practice, it is anticipated that most companies will continue to apply these bright lines for purposes of their internal policies in an effort to drive consistency in their lease classification tests. Finally, it's also important to note that in the new lease accounting standards, there are now five criteria to be assessed with the addition of the "specialized nature that it is expected to have no alternative use to the lessor" criterion. This specialized nature consideration was not included in the previous lease accounting standard.

Similar to the previous lease standard, if any of the criteria are met, it is a finance lease. If none of the criteria are met, it is an operating lease. At the end of the day, since most operating leases are now going on the balance sheet, this classification is more important for subsequent measurement purposes and not whether or not it will be recognized as an asset and liability on an entity's balance sheet.

¶ 107 SUBSEQUENT MEASUREMENT FOR LESSEES

There is no difference in the subsequent measurement requirements for an operating lease versus a finance lease as it relates to the lease liability that is recorded by a lessee in a lease transaction. Therefore, the lease liability is adjusted such that it reflects the present value of all remaining lease payments using the discount rate applied when it was initially measured and recorded. However, the subsequent measurement requirements for the right-of-use asset for an operating lease are very different from those for a finance lease. For a finance lease, the right-of-use asset is economically similar to other nonfinancial assets. As a result, the new lease accounting standards require that this right-of-use asset be measured at cost, net of accumulated amortization, and be amortized on a straight-line basis from the commencement date to the end of the lease term.

¶ 108 PRESENTATION AND DISCLOSURE REQUIREMENTS

From a lessee's perspective, the FASB concluded that a lessee should either present separately in the statement of financial position, or disclose separately in the notes, both finance lease right-of-use assets and operating lease right-of-use assets, separately from other assets. This requirement also holds true for both finance lease liabilities and operating lease liabilities. In other words, entities are prohibited from presenting finance lease and operating lease assets and liabilities within the same line items.

When determining the disclosure requirements for both lessees and lessors, the FASB considered the requirements prescribed within previous lease accounting standards and decisions from the FASB's disclosure framework project. Included within the final lease accounting standards, the FASB prescribed that companies should consider the level of detail necessary to satisfy the disclosure objective as well as how much emphasis to place on various requirements. As you can imagine, the disclosure requirements related to the new lease standard are extensive and a comprehensive discussion of these requirements is beyond the scope of this chapter. Note, though, that these disclosures include requirements related to information about the nature of the company's leases, significant assumptions and judgments, as well as extensive quantitative information.

¶ 109 IMPACT OF THE NEW LEASE STANDARD FOR LESSORS

The FASB noted, based on feedback received from its two exposure drafts as well as other outreach activities, that the lessor accounting model did not need comprehensive improvements. On account of this conclusion, the FASB concluded that changing the model in any significant way would not have produced benefits significant enough to justify the added costs. As a result, the accounting requirements for lessors were largely left unchanged. Accordingly, the majority of operating leases should remain classified as operating leases, and lessors will continue to recognize lease income for those leases on a generally straight-line basis over the lease term.

A lessor's lease can be classified as either a sales-type, direct financing, or operating lease. The requirements for a lessor's lease to be classified as a sales type is the same as those for a lessee classifying a lease as a finance lease. When a lease does not meet any of the finance lease criteria, it is classified as either a direct financing lease or an operating lease. If a lease is determined not to be a direct financing lease, then by default it is considered an operating lease by the lessor.

¶ 110 TRANSITIONING TO THE NEW STANDARD

The new lease accounting standards are effective for public business entities and certain not-for-profit and employee benefit plans for fiscal years beginning after December 15, 2018, including interim periods within those periods. For all other entities, the new standards were originally effective for fiscal years beginning after December 15, 2019, and interim periods within fiscal years beginning after December 15, 2020. However, in October 2019, the FASB approved its August 2019 proposal to grant private companies, not-for-profit organizations, and certain small public companies various effective date delays on the new lease standard. For private and all other entities, this essentially provided them an additional year to fully implement the standard. As a result, while all public business entities have adopted the new lease accounting standard (even those filers that are not a calendar year-end), there are certain private and other entities that may not have adopted the new standard yet.

Additionally, note that subsequent to the first release of the new lease standard in 2016 through ASU 2016-02, a multitude of ASUs were released that clarified certain aspects of the standard as well as provided additional improvements and interpretations. All of these ASUs as well as the impacted areas to the guidance in ASC 842 are available on the FASB.org website.

¶ 111 CHALLENGES AND LESSONS LEARNED FROM THE NEW LEASE STANDARD

A simple Google search of the term "lessons learned from new lease standard" will yield a multitude of articles provided by various organizations and companies that were intimately involved in the new lease accounting standard. Narrowing down the long list of issues and lessons learned to a top 5 or top 10 list is not possible and is subject to significant judgment. Additionally, some of the issues may have impacted only a small minority of entities, whereas others may have been felt by many entities across a great number of industries.

In this section of the chapter, we'll focus primarily on a handful of issues encountered and lessons learned that are applicable to most entities. Again, even though the new lease standard has been adopted by all public business entities, the lessons learned and issues encountered are helpful to understand when the FASB releases the next big update to a major accounting standard. In addition, for those private and other entities that have not yet adopted the new standard, these lessons learned and issues encountered are critical to consider as they start to (hopefully) finalize their adoption plans.

Start Early

As you already know, the new lease standard brought about significant changes to the lease guidance that resulted in billions of dollars being put on the balance sheets of public business entities. For some, the impacts were felt more than others.

One of the first lessons learned with respect to adoption of the new lease standard is to start early. The FASB released the new guidance in the early part of 2016. While this feels like many years at this point, the effective date creeps up more quickly than many expect. Based on the experiences of many public business entities, the process of implementing the new lease accounting standard took longer than first planned.

Although this lesson learned seems obvious in principle, the issues addressed in the subsequent parts of this chapter are what make this suggestion to start early so important. In other words, a majority of the issues encountered in the implementation of the new standard could have been avoided, or at least lessened to a large extent, by starting early.

Understand the Unknown

Companies are not allowed to adopt the new lease standard on a prospective basis. In other words, they don't simply get to apply the new requirements, new classification criteria, and new subsequent measurement and disclosure requirements on a go-forward basis to new arrangements that are concluded to be leases. Instead, lessees and lessors are required to adopt the new lease standard and recognize and measure leases at the beginning of the earliest period presented using a modified retrospective approach. While this transition approach allows for the application of certain optional practical expedients, such as identification and classification of leases that commenced before the effective date, initial direct costs for leases that commenced before the effective date, and the ability to use hindsight in evaluating lessee options to extend or terminate a lease or to purchase the underlying asset, companies are still required to reassess certain arrangements in light of the new guidance.

To put the previous paragraph into appropriate context, the unknown we're talking about here relates to the population of leases. In a perfect accounting world, a company's lease arrangements would be clearly labeled as lease arrangements, and anything not labeled as a lease arrangement would not be classified as a lease. It's not a perfect accounting world, though, and as you'll recall from the definition of a lease and the questions to ask when determining whether an arrangement contains a lease, there may be significant judgment involved in this determination. Said another way, an arrangement that may not appear to be a lease on the surface, and one that was not contemplated to be a lease when it was entered into by a company, may in fact be a lease or contain an embedded lease. For this reason, and given that companies have to apply the new guidance on a modified retrospective basis, they have to first understand their population of leases. Of course, some of a company's leases will be obvious. For example, a lease of an office building is an obvious lease and is likely labeled as such within the contractual agreement. However, other leases under the new definition may not be as obvious. As a result, determining your lease population and engaging in a comprehensive search of your company's contractual arrangements that may or may not contain a lease can be a significant undertaking. This again goes back to the first lesson learned—start early.

Based on its publication titled *Lease Accounting for Private Companies: Lessons Learned from Public Company Implementations*, Deloitte notes the following as it relates to determining your population of leases:

> Finding and documenting these embedded leases can involve considerable time and judgment, including a close look at all operations, identifying areas where embedded leases are more likely to exist, and meeting with relevant stakeholders to understand whether assets are deployed as part of service contracts. An examination of expense activity may also be required, as well as a physical inspection and a legal review to highlight contracts for further evaluation.

Overall, it is unfortunate that many companies may significantly underestimate the time and effort it will take to both collect and organize lease information. In fact, companies may end up surprising themselves at what turns out to be a lease under the new standard. An issue that further compounds this problem is the decentralization of leasing processes. For example, most companies do not have one central department that enters into all new lease arrangements with its vendors and suppliers. If they did, they would be able to focus their population search to this single department and analyze the list of arrangements this department would theoretically be able to provide. Instead, most companies, especially the larger ones with international operations, have more decentralized operations wherein the business units and subsidiaries across the world are entering into arrangements day in and day out. If these arrangements are not being effectively tracked, uncovering them can be a daunting exercise. Again, start early.

Embedded Leases

Another significant challenge, and one that is closely related to the previous discussion around determining the population of leases, is the concept of embedded leases. While this sounds like a complex accounting term, it's rather simple. An embedded lease is simply a lease contained within a larger arrangement. However, finding these embedded leases can require significant time and effort as again, the term "lease" or "embedded lease" is likely not going to jump right out at you when reviewing a contract. Determining the number of embedded leases likely requires, at minimum, a cursory review of nearly every contract as well as further examination of expense activity (i.e., would recurring payments be indicative of a lease arrangement).

Embedded leases can be hiding throughout an organization. For example, they could be found in areas such as information technology contracts, transportation and delivery services, contract manufacturing arrangements, and power purchase arrangements, just to name a few. While it is possible, and sometimes likely, that some of these contracts with these potential embedded leases may not meet all aspects of the new lease definition after reviewing and considering the specific terms, it is imperative that companies perform a thorough analysis to identify and document contracts that may contain embedded leases. By not understanding the full population of its leases, a company can run the risk of material misstatement.

Standardized Lease Data

As previously noted, one of the challenges of the new lease standard is determining your population of leases and embedded leases. However, this is only the first step—albeit a big step—in determining what needs to be recorded upon adoption. Unless your company already has a very robust leasing/procurement process, which maintains a comprehensive listing of the key terms within each lease contract, chances are extracting the needed information from each contract will prove challenging. Still, once that lease data is successfully extracted, having a software solution in place to track that information over time will prove to be another significant challenge. While accountants certainly stretch Microsoft Excel to its limits in some ways, for most complex organizations, spreadsheet tracking will not be sufficient as far as a long-term solution. Again, going back to our first point, start early.

The new lease standard requires that companies identify certain critical dates in a lease term, amounts paid under the respective lease terms, as well as other critical information about the right of use prescribed by the lease contract. However, the challenge in extracting this information is the fact that not all lease arrangements are standard. While there are certainly some boilerplate provisions included within most company's lease arrangements, many of these arrangements are of a unique nature. For example, some lease agreements may contain both complex and unique provisions specific to a company or specific to its industry. Additionally, some lease contracts may also be in a foreign language. One of the most challenging nuances regarding a company's lease contracts is the potential for a significant number of amendments to a very old master agreement. Locating all of these amendments and understanding how they impact the original terms and conditions of the original agreement can prove to be a significant undertaking.

In the previously referenced Deloitte publication, the company notes the following regarding this challenging area:

> If suitable lease data does not currently exist, companies will need to abstract required data from the underlying lease contract(s), which can be a significant and labor-intensive task. Artificial intelligence (AI) tools exist to assist in abstraction and should be considered wherever possible, but the technology has limitations, especially when dealing with older lease contracts. As such, AI generally can aid human effort, but not replace it altogether. People must still review the output, execute quality control procedures, and consider additional fields to abstract outside the lease contract.

System Solutions for Lease Tracking and Reporting

While the new lease accounting standard made for a significant undertaking for companies, it also created opportunities for others in their development of lease accounting software. As we alluded to earlier, tracking all of the newfound lease data within Microsoft Excel is probably not a long-term solution. Although this may be a temporary solution and will likely be used when building out your initial lease population, it is not a long-term solution that companies can effectively rely on.

A simple Google search for "lease management software" will yield plenty of results. Software solutions such as Visual Lease, LeaseQuery, Leasecake, Spacebase, Nakisa Lease Administration, and ProLease commonly come up when searching. Some of these software solutions you may have heard of, and others you likely have not. These software solutions range from simple stand-alone programs with significant manual inputs required by the end user to large-scale sophisticated systems that seamlessly integrate with a company's larger ERP (enterprise resource planning) or GL (general ledger) system. Lease management software also varies depending on the industry. A company that is heavily involved in the leasing business (e.g., a commercial real estate company that owns buildings and leases them), is probably already using a certain type of lease management software for its leasing activities. However, it is also unlikely that this current software solution will have everything the company needs to account for all the requirements and necessary data to apply the amendments of the new lease accounting standard.

The new lease standard requires significantly more data and additional calculations in order to develop the needed accounting journal entries and respective disclosures. Because of this, manual processes around leasing activities are less practical for tracking lease modifications, modeling different valuation scenarios, and preparing journal entries and disclosures. As a result, early in the implementation process, companies need to consider potential technology solutions in order to effectively track their new and existing leases. At the risk of stating the obvious, companies also need to consider the costs associated with acquiring this new software as well as additional costs to customize it for their use. While some of the lease accounting software is fairly off-the-shelf in nature, costs will undoubtedly be incurred to customize it for a company's specific operations.

The key point is that many companies that have already adopted the new lease accounting have discovered that it took longer for the expected new software to be fully operational. Again, start early, and don't discount the fact that the time to acquire (or develop) and customize a new lease management software may be significant in relation to the overall lease standard implementation process.

Incremental Borrowing Rate Issues

Within the new lease standard, the term *incremental borrowing rate* is defined as " . . . the rate of interest that a lessee would have to pay to borrow on a collateralized basis over a similar term an amount equal to the lease payments in a similar economic environment." Under the new lease standard, lessees are required to use this incremental borrowing rate in order to record leases on its balance sheet. However, not all companies have the same incremental borrowing rate. In fact, one company may have multiple incremental borrowing rates depending on different lease terms and lease currencies. Furthermore, these incremental borrowing rates are not stagnant over time. Some public companies assumed incorrectly that obtaining information needed to develop the incremental borrowing rate would be a straightforward exercise in the implementation roadmap. These companies soon realized that the processes needed to obtain these rates were significantly more complex than anticipated.

When developing the incremental borrowing rate, companies will often start with some type of base rate that appropriately reflects their current cost of borrowing. From this rate, they will then likely make adjustments as needed to reflect consideration of factors such as lease-specific factors, company-specific factors, credit risk, and whether the arrangements involve collateralized versus uncollateralized terms. One additional complexity in the area of developing an incremental borrowing rate relates to subsidiaries within the company. Refer to the following excerpt from Deloitte's publication *Demystifying the New Leasing Standard*:

It is important to note that subsidiaries may not necessarily default to using rates reflective of the parents' credit standing—generally speaking, a subsidiary should only take into account parent credit if the parent guarantees the lease or the lessor otherwise had reason to consider the parent's credit when negotiating the lease. Accordingly, the organizational structure may necessitate separate consideration of the credit quality of certain subsidiaries in addition to that of the parent. Further, if a company is party to leases denominated in foreign currencies, additional adjustments to the established base rates will need to be considered in order to capture any applicable currency and/or political risks inherent in each jurisdiction. For a multinational, the result is likely to include a variety of IBR curves that reflect different combinations of credit, currency, and political risks that will be applied to leases based on their key characteristics.

As you can note from the excerpt above, for large multinational companies with a significant number of subsidiaries, the chances of having a single established incremental borrowing rate is likely remote. However, the FASB does note in its Basis for Conclusion that it " . . . considered that, in some cases, it might be reasonable for a subsidiary to use a parent entity or group's incremental borrowing rate as the discount rate. Depending on the terms and conditions of the lease and the corresponding negotiations, the parent entity's incremental borrowing rate may be the most appropriate rate to use as a practical means of reflecting the interest rate in the contract, assuming the implicit rate is not readily determinable."

Again, going back to our first lesson learned, start early! While companies that have already adopted the new standard have been faced with significant challenges in this area, companies that are soon to adopt can lessen those challenges by adopting a consistent methodology for developing their incremental borrowing rate.

Specific to private companies, there is some additional leniency afforded in this area through a practical expedient offered with the new lease standard. More specifically, the new lease standard includes a practical expedient for lessees that are private companies that allows an accounting policy election for the initial and subsequent measurement of all liabilities to make lease payments. To that end, the FASB allows a private company to elect to use a risk-free rate determined at lease commencement using a period comparable with the term of the lease, so long as it applies this methodology to all leases and to disclose that it has elected to use the practical expedient. The benefit of this practical expedient is that it permits a private company to use a single, risk-free rate, determined at lease commencement, to discount leases with similar but not identical lease terms.

COVID-19 Impacts

One of the more recent post-implementation issues related to the new leasing standard relates to the COVID-19 pandemic. Given the significant amount of business disruptions and challenges that are severely affecting the global economy caused by the COVID-19 pandemic, there are many lessors that will be providing (or have already provided) lease concessions to lessees for a significant number of lease contracts. These lease concessions vary in form from company to company, but most commonly involve either payment forgiveness or deferral of payments. This is an area that the FASB has commented on in April 2020 given that the number of contracts for which concessions are granted is expected to be substantial for many lessors and lessees. In response to these events, the FASB staff developed a Q&A to respond to some frequently asked questions about accounting for lease concessions related to the effects of the COVID-19 pandemic.

You're probably asking yourself how this presents itself as a post-implementation issue. Note that subsequent changes to lease payments that are not prescribed within an original lease contract are generally accounted for as lease modifications. In other words, it is highly unlikely that any existing lease considered the economic effects from a global pandemic such as COVID-19. The FASB further notes that some contracts may contain explicit or implicit enforceable rights and obligations that require lease concessions if certain circumstances arise that are beyond the control of the parties to the contract. For example, if a lease contract provides enforceable rights and obligations for concessions in the contract and no changes are made to that contract, the concessions are not accounted under the lease modification guidance. However, if concessions granted by lessors are beyond the enforceable rights and obligations in the contract, companies would generally account for those concessions in accordance with the lease modification guidance.

Before we dive too deep into the FASB's Q&A that addresses the impacts from COVID-19 on the application of the lease modifications guidance, let's first level set on the overall requirements with respect to lease modifications.

The FASB ASC Master Glossary defines a *lease modification* as "a change to the terms and conditions of a contract that results in a change in the scope of or the consideration for a lease." As an example, a lease modification could be a change to the terms and conditions of the contract that adds or terminates the right to use one or more underlying assets or extends or shortens the contractual lease term. Further to this point, in situations when a lease modification occurs, a company has to determine whether the lease modification will be accounted for as a separate contract or as a change to the existing contract. Specifically, a company is required to account for a modification to a lease contract as a separate contract when *both* of the following conditions are present:

- The modification grants the lessee an additional right-of-use not included in the original lease.
- The lease payments increase commensurate with the stand-alone price for the additional right-of-use, adjusted for the circumstances of the particular contract.

If the lease modification is not accounted for as a separate contract, then a company is required to reassess the classification of the lease as of the effective date of the modification based on the modified terms and conditions. Herein lie the potential impacts from the lease concessions; if the contract is not accounted for as a separate contract, then a company would be required to reassess the lease classification as of the effective date of the modification based on the new terms and conditions. For a company that has granted a significant number of concessions, this could be quite an undertaking.

To provide additional clarity on this topic, the FASB published a Q&A that addressed some of the complexities related to these lease concessions and how companies are expected to apply the lease modifications guidance. While we won't present a full overview of all of the Q&A provided, a summary of the excerpts and key takeaways from the publication are included below. You're encouraged to review the full text of the Q&A available on FASB.org.

Question 1: Are lease concessions related to the effects of the COVID-19 pandemic required to be accounted for in accordance with the lease modification guidance in Topic 842 and Topic 840?

Answer: *The FASB staff believes that it would be acceptable for entities to make an election to account for lease concessions related to the effects of the COVID-19 pandemic consistent with how those concessions would be accounted for under Topic 842 and Topic 840 as* *though enforceable rights and obligations for those concessions existed. This election is available for concessions related to the effects of the COVID-19 pandemic that do not result in a substantial increase in the rights of the lessor or the obligations of the lessee.*

Question 2: Is an entity precluded from accounting for lease concessions related to the effects of the COVID-19 pandemic by applying the lease modification guidance in Topic 842 and Topic 840?

Answer: *No. An entity may account for lease concessions related to the effects of the COVID-19 pandemic in accordance with the lease modification accounting guidance in Topic 842 and Topic 840.*

Question 3: Does an entity have to account for all lease concessions related to the effects of the COVID-19 pandemic either (a) as if the enforceable rights and obligations to those concessions existed in the original contract or (b) in accordance with the lease modification guidance in Topic 842 and Topic 840?

Answer: *No. However, entities should apply Topic 842 consistently to leases with similar characteristics and in similar circumstances.*

Question 4: Should an entity provide disclosures about lease concessions related to the effects of the COVID-19 pandemic?

Answer: *Yes. An entity should provide disclosures about material concessions granted or received and the accounting effects.*

STUDY QUESTIONS

---

1. The new leasing standard superseded which of the following ASC Topics?

    a. ASC 840

    b. ASC 845

    c. ASC 605

    d. ASC 250

2. Which of the following identifies the first question to be considered when determining whether an arrangement contains a lease?

    a. Does the customer have rights to operate the asset?

    b. Did the customer design the asset?

    c. Is there an asset identified in the contract?

    d. Does the customer obtain substantially all of the economic benefits from the arrangement?

3. Which of the following is a correct statement regarding lease concessions and modifications as a result of COVID-19?

    a. The FASB has remained silent on the impacts of COVID-19 with respect to lease concessions and modifications.

    b. The SEC published a Q&A regarding COVID-19 impacts to lease modifications.

    c. Entities are not required to provide disclosures about material lease concessions related to the effects of the COVID-19 pandemic.

    d. If the lease modification is not accounted for as a separate contract, then a company is required to reassess the classification of the lease.

¶ 112 OVERVIEW OF THE NEW CREDIT LOSSES STANDARD

At this point in the chapter, we will now shift gears to discuss the new credit losses standard and some of the lessons learned and post-implementation issues. Similar to the previous section related to the new lease standard, we begin this part of the chapter by going over some of the fundamental information and guidance included within the new credit losses standard.

In 2016, the FASB issued final guidance that significantly changes how entities will measure credit losses for most financial assets and certain other instruments that aren't measured at fair value through net income. By issuing the new amendments outlined in ASC Topic 326, the FASB responded to criticism that current accounting and reporting guidance delays recognition of credit losses. As a result, the new standard will replace the current "incurred loss" approach with an "expected loss" model for instruments measured at amortized cost and requires entities to record allowances for available-for-sale debt securities rather than reduce the carrying amount, as they do today under the other-than-temporary impairment (OTTI) model. The new standard will also simplify the accounting model for purchased credit-impaired debt securities and loans.

The FASB notes that the main objective of the ASU is to provide financial statement users with more decision-useful information about the expected credit losses on financial instruments and other commitments to extend credit held by a reporting entity at each reporting date. In order to achieve this objective, the amendments replace the current incurred loss impairment methodology with an updated methodology that reflects expected credit losses and requires entities to consider a broader range of reasonable and supportable information with respect to credit loss estimates. More specifically, the ASU affects the following two types of assets:

- Assets measured at amortized cost
- Available-for-sale debt securities

With respect to assets measured at amortized costs, the amendments within the ASU require a financial asset (or a group of financial assets) measured at amortized cost basis to be presented at the net amount expected to be collected. The net amount expected to be collected is determined by using a valuation account that is deducted from the amortized cost basis. Regarding available-for-sale debt securities, the amendments in the ASU require that credit losses relating to these types of financial instruments should be recorded through an allowance for credit losses.

¶ 113 ASSETS MEASURED AT AMORTIZED COST

Current accounting principles include multiple credit impairment objectives for certain financial instruments. As we previously mentioned, the current objectives generally delayed recognition of the full amount of credit losses until the loss was probable of occurring. Based on the FASB's summary of the ASU, the FASB noted that the amendments in this ASU are an improvement because they eliminate the probable initial recognition threshold in current GAAP (generally accepted accounting principles) and, instead, reflect an entity's current estimate of all expected credit losses. Previously, when credit losses were measured under GAAP, an entity generally considered only past events and current conditions in measuring the incurred loss. As a result of this ASU, the changes broaden the information that an entity must consider in developing its expected credit loss estimate for assets measured either collectively or individually. Furthermore, the FASB notes that the use of forecasted information incorporates more timely information in the estimate of expected credit loss, which will be more decision useful to users of the financial statements.

¶ 114 AVAILABLE-FOR-SALE DEBT SECURITIES

Currently, credit losses on available-for-sale debt securities are required to be measured and presented as a write-down. The amendments in this ASU do not change the requirement to measure these credit losses; however, the amendments require that the losses be presented as an allowance rather than as a write-down. The FASB notes that this is an improvement to current accounting principles because an entity will be able to record reversals of credit losses (in situations in which the estimate of credit losses declines) in current period net income, which in turn should align the income statement recognition of credit losses with the reporting period in which changes occur. This is in contrast with current GAAP, which prohibits reflecting those improvements in current period earnings.

¶ 115 INITIAL MEASUREMENT OF EXPECTED LOSSES

As should be clear by now, the allowance for expected credit losses represents the portion of the amortized cost of a financial asset that an entity does not expect to collect. The FASB further notes that an allowance for credit losses may be determined using various methods. In other words, it does not require a single method be used for estimating credit losses. The acceptable methods provided within the new credit losses standard include the following:

- Discounted cash flow methods
- Loss-rate methods
- Roll-rate methods
- Probability-of-default methods
- Methods that use an aging schedule

In its Basis for Conclusions, the FASB notes that any approach to estimating the collectability of financial assets is subjective, which is why it has permitted entities to estimate expected credit losses using various methods. This is because the FASB believes entities manage credit risk differently and should have flexibility to best report their expectations.

While the FASB does not prescribe a specific method be used by all entities, it should be noted that the measurement requirements can vary depending on whether an entity elects to use a discounted cash flow method or not. For example, if an entity estimates expected credit losses using a discounted cash flow method, the entity should discount expected cash flows at the financial asset's effective interest rate. Alternatively, if an entity estimates expected credit losses using a method other than a discounted cash flow method, the allowance for credit losses should reflect an entity's expected credit losses of the amortized cost basis of the financial asset(s) as of the reporting date.

The actual estimation of credit losses, no matter the type of model utilized by an entity, can be highly judgmental and will undoubtedly be based on entity-specific factors such as the following (not an exhaustive list):

- The definition of default for default-based statistics
- The approach to measuring the historical loss amount for loss-rate statistics
- The approach to determining the appropriate historical period for estimating expected credit loss statistics
- The approach to adjusting historical credit loss information to reflect current conditions and reasonable and supportable forecasts that are different from conditions existing in the historical period
- The methods of utilizing historical experience
- The method of adjusting loss statistics for recoveries

¶ 116 SUBSEQUENT MEASUREMENT OF EXPECTED LOSSES

At each reporting date, an entity is required to record an allowance for credit losses on financial assets (including purchased financial assets with credit deterioration). As a result, an entity should compare its current estimate of expected credit losses with the estimate of expected credit losses previously recorded. By doing this, an entity should report in net income (as a credit loss expense or a reversal of credit loss expense) the amount necessary to adjust the allowance for credit losses for management's current estimate of expected credit losses on financial asset(s).

¶ 117 FINANCIAL STATEMENT DISCLOSURES

The required disclosures with respect to credit losses of financial instruments measured at amortized cost, as well as available-for-sale debt securities, are prescribed to accomplish three specific objectives. This includes providing information that enables users of an entity's financial statements to understand each of the following:

- The credit risk inherent in a portfolio and how management monitors the credit quality of the portfolio
- Management's estimate of expected credit losses
- Changes in the estimate of expected credit losses that have taken place during the period

In its Basis for Conclusions, the FASB notes that while it chose to retain many existing financial statement disclosures about an entity's allowance for credit losses, the change from an incurred to an expected loss model introduces the need for additional disclosures, most notably those about the inputs used to estimate expected credit losses. Furthermore, requiring an entity to use expected loss data when determining expected credit losses will require the entity to incorporate new types of information into its measurement of expected credit losses and increase the significance of forward-looking information and its judgment in calculating the allowance for expected credit losses on its financial assets.

Although we will not discuss these disclosures in additional detail, note that the disclosure requirements outlined within ASC 326 are broken out among the following major categories for those financial instruments measured at amortized cost:

- Credit quality information
- Allowance for credit losses
- Past-due status
- Nonaccrual status
- Purchased financial assets with credit deterioration
- Collateral-dependent financial assets
- Off-balance-sheet credit exposures

For those available-for-sale debt securities, the disclosures are broken out among the following categories:

- Available-for-sale debt securities in unrealized loss positions without an allowance for credit losses
- Allowance for credit losses
- Purchased financial assets with credit deterioration

¶ 118 IMPLEMENTATION OF THE NEW CREDIT LOSSES STANDARD

For public business entities that are U.S. Securities and Exchange Commission (SEC) filers, the new credit losses standard is effective for fiscal years beginning after December 15, 2019, including interim periods within those fiscal years. As a result, those public business entity SEC filers that are calendar-year filers have only recently adopted the new credit losses standard starting in Q1 2020 (unless they early adopted). For other public business entity SEC filers with a fiscal year end, they may or may not have adopted the new credit losses standard at the writing of this chapter.

Originally, the new credit losses standard was set to be adopted by smaller reporting entities and other private entities generally one or two years after public business entities. However, in October 2019, the FASB approved its August 2019 proposal to grant private companies, not-for-profit organizations, and certain small public companies various effective date delays on its credit losses standards. As a result, all other public business entities that are not SEC filers, as well as private entities and all others, are now required to adopt the new standard in January 2023 (instead of January 2021). For all entities, the new credit losses standard is required to be adopted using a modified retrospective approach.

On account of the above, it is likely that at the time of this writing, only public business entities who are SEC filers have adopted the new standard (notwithstanding those entities that early adopted). As a result, there is likely a limited amount of post-implementation issues and lessons as compared to the previously discussed lease standard. However, we will touch on a few key issues and areas to be aware of in the following sections of this chapter.

Start Early

For entities that have not yet adopted the new credit losses standard, the delayed implementation date may seem like a lifetime away. However, don't let this fool you. The new credit losses standard is likely one of the largest changes from the FASB within the last several years. The impacts of the new standard should not be underestimated.

Similar to the previous discussion on the new lease accounting standard, it is important to start early in the implementation process. For some companies, especially those that have very sophisticated reserve allowance models for their financial instruments, the implementation of the standard may focus more on tailoring their documentation to ensure it is appropriately aligned with the new requirements in ASC 326. For other companies that do not have this level of sophistication in their current reserve methodology, or do not have consistent methodologies that are also well documented, the implementation of the new standard can prove to be very challenging and time-consuming.

One of the important points to note is that while current accounting standards require an allowance for credit losses that is only expected to incur over the next 12 months, the new credit losses standard removes this probable loss threshold and instead requires a lifetime credit loss allowance to be established on day one of each credit loss exposure. This will undoubtedly result in the need for new and more complex models for estimating credit losses.

At the risk of stating the obvious, the amount of disclosures under the new credit losses standard will increase significantly. While a good number of the previous disclosures have been preserved in principle, there are increased disclosures required around assumptions and methodology choices, as well as any adjustments to the process for developing credit loss estimates.

Transition Resource Group for Credit Losses

Unlike the new lease standard, the FASB set up a Transition Resource Group for purposes of the new credit losses standard. A similar group was also set up a few years back with respect to the new revenue recognition standard. The group's purpose is:

- To solicit, analyze, and discuss stakeholder issues arising from implementation of the new guidance

- To inform the FASB about those implementation issues, which will help the Board determine what, if any, action will be needed to address those issues

- To provide a forum for stakeholders to learn about the new guidance from others involved with implementation

This Transition Resource Group has been involved in certain post-issuance activities. One of these relates to the acceptability of using a weighted-average maturity model for purposes of developing an estimate of expected credit losses. The FASB notes in its Q&A that this method uses an average annual charge-off rate that contains loss content over several vintages and is used as a foundation for estimating the credit loss content for the remaining balances of financial assets in a pool at the balance sheet date. In its Q&A, the FASB published a question about whether this method is acceptable for determining an allowance for credit losses. In short, the FASB noted that it believes that this method is one of many methods that could be used to estimate an allowance for credit losses for less complex financial asset pools. Refer to the complete Q&A on the FASB.org website for additional information on this topic.

Another topic addressed by the Transition Resource Group related to the new credit losses standard relates to developing estimates of expected credit losses on financial assets. In short, the new standard contains a requirement of applying a reasonable and supportable forecast and, if applicable, reverting to historical loss information if an entity is unable to forecast credit losses over the estimated life of the instrument, when measuring expected credit losses. The FASB notes that questions have been posed on acceptable approaches for determining reasonable and supportable forecasts and techniques for reverting to historical loss information when developing an estimate of expected credit losses on financial assets. Similar to the previous Q&A regarding the lease concession impacts from COVID-19, we've provided some key excerpts of the Q&A related to the new credit losses standard below. As before, these are only excerpts (with certain extraneous detail removed), and you should refer to the full text of the Q&A available on the FASB.org website.

Question 1: Does the application of the word *forecast* infer computer-based modeling analysis is required?

Answer: *No, developing forecasts does not require an entity to perform computer-based modeling. Topic 326 allows a quantitative or a qualitative adjustment to be made when assessing current conditions and reasonable and supportable forecasts.*

Question 2: If an entity's actual credit losses differ from its estimate of expected credit losses, is it required to modify its forecasting methodology?

Answer: *The Board notes that estimates of expected credit losses often will not predict with precision actual future events. The objective of the new standard is to present the best estimate of the net amount expected to be collected on financial assets. The Board understands that there generally is a range of reasonable outcomes and, therefore, expects there to be differences between estimates of expected credit losses and actual credit losses.*

Question 3: Can an entity's process for determining expected credit losses consider only historical information?

Answer: *No. The guidance states that an entity should not rely solely on past events to estimate expected credit losses.*

Question 10: Should an entity reevaluate its reasonable and supportable forecast period each reporting period?

Answer: *Yes. An entity should consider the appropriateness of its reasonable and supportable forecast period, as well as other judgments applied in developing estimates of expected credit losses each reporting period.*

Additional Guidance from the SEC (ASU 2020-02)

In February 2020, the FASB released ASU 2020-02 (*Amendments to SEC Paragraphs Pursuant to SEC Staff Accounting Bulletin No. 119 and Update to SEC Section on Effective Date Related to Accounting Standards Update No. 2016-02*). Notwithstanding the effective date changes related to the new lease standard, this ASU included the text from the SEC's SAB Topic 6.M, *Financial Reporting Release No. 28 (Accounting for Loan Losses by Registrants Engaged in Lending Activities Subject to FASB ASC Topic 326)*. Simply put, this ASU codified that information within the FASB ASC.

This additional guidance, as you've likely already noted, is applicable to SEC filers/registrants. However, some of the clarifications through the SAB Topic's Q&A are helpful for those filers that have not yet adopted the new credit losses standard.

One of the first questions posed relates to the factors or elements that the SEC normally would expect a company to consider when developing (or subsequently performing an assessment of) its methodology for determining its allowance for credit losses under GAAP. In its response, the SEC notes that it would ". . . expect a registrant to have a systematic methodology to address the development, governance, and documentation to determine its provision and allowance for credit losses." Furthermore, the SEC believes that ". . . an entity's management should review, on a periodic basis, whether its methodology for determining its allowance for credit losses is appropriate."

Another topic addressed by the SEC relates to the documentation requirements related to a company's methodology for estimating credit losses. At the risk of stating the obvious, the SEC believes that "appropriate written supporting documentation for the provision and allowance for credit losses facilitates review of the allowance for credit losses process and reported amounts, builds discipline and consistency into the allowance for credit losses methodology, and helps to evaluate whether relevant factors are appropriately considered in the allowance analysis." More specifically, the SEC normally would expect companies to maintain written supporting documentation for the following decisions and processes:

- Policies and procedures over the systems and controls that maintain an appropriate allowance for credit losses
- Allowance for credit losses methodology and key judgments, including the data used, assessment of risk, and identification of significant assumptions in the allowance estimation process
- Summary or consolidation of the allowance for credit losses balance
- Validation of the allowance for credit losses methodology
- Periodic adjustments to the allowance for credit losses

In addition to the documentation requirements related to a company's methodology for its credit loss process, the SEC also commented on its expectation around the documentation needed for purposes of actually developing an expected credit loss. In its Q&A, the SEC indicated that it normally would expect a company to demonstrate in its documentation that the loss measurement methods and assumptions used to estimate the allowance for credit losses for its loan portfolio are determined in accordance with GAAP as of the financial statement date. This would include, more specifically, the estimated credit losses for each portfolio segment.

COVID-19 Impacts

As you know, the impacts from COVID-19 are far-reaching across many different financial reporting and disclosures areas. For some companies, the impacts may be broad and significant, whereas for others, the impacts may be narrower in nature. We already discussed COVID-19 impacts with respect to leasing; now we'll touch on this topic as it relates to the new credit losses standard.

Since the new credit losses standard has been adopted by some entities and not by others, companies are using different areas of GAAP in connection with the pandemic. For example, for those entities that have adopted the new credit losses standard, they will apply the requirements within ASC 326 (compared to those who have not adopted and would look to guidance in ASC 310, *Receivables*).

Companies that are currently applying the new credit losses standard requirements are required to consider reasonable and supportable forecasts of future economic conditions in their estimate of expected credit losses. Because of the heightened uncertainty surrounding the COVID-19 economic impacts, the effects of the pandemic could change their forecast of future economic conditions significantly. For example, the decrease in demand and the negative impacts to supply chains across many industries, which in turn results in some borrowers being unable to repay their invoices/obligations when due, can cause extreme changes in an entity's estimated credit losses.

In its March 2020 publication *Accounting and Reporting Considerations for the Effects of the Coronavirus Outbreak*, EY notes the following:

> We expect that it may be difficult to determine the economic effect of the COVID-19 pandemic since historical data may not include the effects of similar events. Further, affected companies should consider whether the effects increase the likelihood of reasonably expected troubled debt restructurings (TDRs) since it may be necessary to modify a borrower's payment terms (including providing a borrower more time to pay its debt).

The firm further notes that companies should consider highlighting these risks in their qualitative and quantitative disclosures about credit risk and the allowance for credit losses, and should also consider the disclosures related to the basis of inputs and assumptions and estimation techniques used.

¶ 119 CONCLUSION

The new lease and the new credit losses standards were significant ASUs released by the FASB within the recent years. Entities that have not adopted these standards should ensure that they are taking stock of the issues facing those entities that have already adopted the standards and plan for these issues accordingly in their own implementation plans.

STUDY QUESTIONS

4. If an entity estimates expected credit losses using a discounted cash flow method, the entity should discount expected cash flows using which of the following?

    a. Weighted average cost of capital

    b. Effective interest rate

    c. LIBOR rate

    d. Cost of equity

5. Which of the following identifies one of the categories of financial statement disclosures for available-for-sale debt securities?

    a. Available-for-sale debt securities in unrealized loss positions without an allowance for credit losses

    b. Past-due status

    c. Nonaccrual status

    d. Collateral-dependent financial assets

6. Which of the following identifies the new effective date of the credit losses standard for calendar-year private companies?

    a. January 2020

    b. January 2021

    c. January 2022

    d. January 2023

MODULE 1: TOP ACCOUNTING ISSUES— CHAPTER 2: Complying with the Updated Revenue Recognition Standard – Topic 606

¶ 201 WELCOME

This chapter outlines the five step revenue recognition model and relevant application for proper compliance with Accounting Standards Update No. 2014-09, *Revenue from Contracts with Customers (Topic 606)*. Although on the surface these steps seem simplistic, there are many considerations to be applied within each step. Considerations can be related to an entities specific processes, industry characteristics as well as contract characteristics.

¶ 202 LEARNING OBJECTIVES

Upon completion of this chapter, you will be able to:

- Identify effective dates for the updated revenue recognition standard
- Explain the need for the updated revenue recognition standard
- Recognize and apply the updated revenue recognition core principles and the five-step revenue recognition model
- Identify the impact of the updated revenue recognition standard on various revenue concepts
- Describe the impact of the revenue recognition standard on various industries

¶ 203 INTRODUCTION

On May 28, 2014, the Financial Accounting Standards Board (FASB) completed its revenue recognition project. It issued Accounting Standards Update (ASU) No. 2014-09, *Revenue from Contracts with Customers (Topic 606)*. The guidance establishes principles to report useful information to users of financial statements about the nature, timing, and uncertainty of revenue from contracts with customers. The standard affects all entities (public, private, and not-for-profit) that have contracts with customers. Exclusions to the standard include:

- Leases accounted for under FASB Accounting Standards Codification (ASC) 840, *Leases*
- Insurance contracts accounted for under FASB ASC 944, *Financial Services—Insurance*
- Most financial instruments and guarantees (other than product or service warranties)

As a result of the updated standard, transaction and industry-specific revenue recognition guidance previously applied is eliminated. It is replaced with a principle-based approach for determining revenue recognition for contracts with customers. The new standard requires significantly more financial statement disclosures than under the previous standard.

¶ 204 EFFECTIVE DATES

The effective dates of ASU No. 2014-09 vary depending on an entity's status as a public company, non-public company, or other organization, including not-for-profits. A public entity has certain characteristics and includes the following:

- A public business organization whose stock is traded on the financial exchanges

- A not-for-profit organization that has issued, or is a conduit bond obligor for, securities that are traded, listed, or quoted on a financial exchange or an over-the-counter market

- An employee benefit plan that files or furnishes financial statements to the Securities and Exchange Commission (SEC)

For public entities, the updated standard is effective for annual reporting periods beginning after December 15, 2017, including interim reporting periods within that reporting period. For nonpublic companies and other organizations, compliance with the standard was originally set for annual reporting periods beginning after December 15, 2018. However, in May 2020, the FASB voted to extend, by one year, the effective date to all nonpublic entities that have not yet issued their financial statements.

¶ 205 OVERVIEW OF THE UPDATED STANDARD

One of the reasons the FASB decided to overhaul the prior standard was that previously GAAP included more than 100 revenue recognition concepts and numerous requirements for particular industries or transactions. The new guidance utilizes a principle-based approach. It focuses on the assets and liabilities created when an entity enters into, and performs, under a contract. The updated revenue recognition standard:

- Provides a more robust framework for addressing revenue issues as they arise

- Increases comparability across industries and capital markets

- Requires better disclosure so investors and other users of financial statements better understand the economics behind the numbers

- Replaces existing accounting guidance for construction contracts, including methods such as the percentage-of-completion method

According to the FASB, the core principle of the updated guidance is that:

"An entity should recognize revenue to depict the transfer of promised goods or services to customers in an amount that reflects the consideration to which the entity expects to be entitled to in exchange for those goods or services."

Under the previous standard, "risk and reward" often drove the determination of revenue recognition.

Significant judgment is required by entities and auditors when applying the principles in the new guidance. Although the risk and reward concept remains important, it is no longer the main determinant for when revenue is recognized. Under the updated standard, transfer of "control" to the customer is the driving determinant in evaluating the appropriateness of revenue recognition.

The updated standard will have an impact on revenue recognition for all companies. Companies that sell products and services in a bundle or engage in major projects could see significant changes in the timing of revenue recognition. Industries that are likely to experience the most changes include telecommunications, aerospace, construction, asset management, real estate, and software.

¶ 206 FIVE-STEP MODEL

Entities applying the updated revenue recognition standard to contracts with customers will follow five steps. These steps will be discussed in detail in this chapter:

- Step One: Identify the contract with the customer

- Step Two: Identify performance obligations

- Step Three: Determine the transaction price

- Step Four: Allocate the transaction price to the performance obligations

- Step Five: Recognize revenue when each performance obligation is satisfied

Organizations that have implemented or plan to implement the new standard require a proactive approach. Preparation includes taking the following actions:

- Ensure a strong evaluation of the information systems needed to adopt the standard. Having a centralized contract management system is important.

- Develop and implement the necessary internal controls.

- Understand the likely impact on financial results.

- Develop internal and external communication plans so interested parties can understand trends.

- Analyze and implement changes in sales or pricing strategies.

- Determine if any corporate policies tied to revenue (e.g., sales commissions and compensation plans) need to be revised.

¶ 207 IMPACT OF THE UPDATED REVENUE RECOGNITION STANDARD

The following chart summarizes the impact of the new revenue recognition guidance versus the previous guidance.

ASU 2014-09 Versus Previous Guidance	
Previous Guidance	**New Guidance**
Provided numerous requirements for recognizing revenue.	Provides *consistent principles* for recognizing revenue regardless of industry or geography.
Most companies provided limited information about revenue contracts within their financial statement disclosures (an exception may be in disclosures in accounting policies and segment reporting).	Guidance requires a cohesive set of *disclosure requirements* intended to provide users of the financial statements with information about the organization's contracts with customers.
Performance obligation concept: In many contracts, goods or services were not deemed to be distinct revenue generating transactions when in fact the promises may have represented separate obligations of the entity and customer.	**Performance obligation concept:** Organizations will: • Identify each of the goods or services promised to a customer, • Determine whether they represent performance obligations, and • Recognize revenue when or as each performance obligation is satisfied.

| ASU 2014-09 Versus Previous Guidance ||
Previous Guidance	New Guidance
Multiple-element arrangements (when a vendor agrees to provide more than one product or a combination of products/services to a customer in an arrangement) limited the amount of consideration allocated to a delivered element to the amount not contingent on delivering future goods or services.	The transaction price is allocated to each performance obligation on the basis of the stand-alone selling price. An exception may occur when a discount/variable amount is related entirely to one or more of the performance obligations.
Accounting for variable consideration (discounts, rebates, refunds, credits, price concessions, incentives, performance bonuses, penalties, and other similar items) differed significantly across industries.	There is a *single model* to consider variable consideration including rebates, discounts, bonuses, and right of return. Variable consideration is part of the transaction price to the extent it is probable that a significant reversal in the amount of cumulative revenue recognized will not occur.

¶ 208 STEP ONE: IDENTIFY THE CONTRACT

Now we will review each of the five steps of the updated revenue recognition model in detail. The first step is to identify the contract. ASC 606-10-05-4 defines a contract broadly as an "agreement between two or more parties that creates enforceable rights and obligations." A contract with a customer must meet several important criteria:

- The contract must have commercial substance.
- The promised goods and services must be identified and approved.
- The payment terms must be identified.

What is commercial substance? A business transaction is said to have commercial substance when it is expected that the future cash flows of a business will change as a result of the transaction.

Another important concept is whether a contract is enforceable. Enforceability is a matter of law and varies between types of customers, jurisdictions, and industries. Several common-law requirements generally must be met for a contract to exist. The common-law elements of a contract include:

- An agreement must exist and have been approved by all parties. The agreement can be written, verbal, or implied.
- Consideration must be exchanged. Consideration is anything of value, including from a future action.
- Capacity to enter into a valid contract must exist. To have capacity, a person must be of sound mind and have reached the age of majority (usually the age of 18 in the United States).

Regarding approval of the contract, the parties to the contract have to approve the contract and be committed to perform. All relevant factors should be considered when determining if the other party is willing to perform. Questions to consider might include:

- Are there termination clauses in the contract?
- Do you have historical experience with similar customers, and does that experience tell you whether this customer is reliable or might not pay?
- What is the customer's ability to perform? For example, a customer that is a new restaurant business might experience a high failure rate in its first few years. Entities must evaluate whether a customer will be able to fulfill the contract.

Other contract requirements per the updated standard include:

- An entity must identify each party's rights regarding the goods or services that are going to be transferred within the contract. If an entity cannot determine its customer's rights or its own rights, it will not be able to identify what performance obligations are within the contract. ASC 606 cannot be applied until the parties specify their rights and obligations, regardless of whether a contract has been approved.

- An entity must also identify the payment terms for the goods or services to be transferred in order to be able to calculate the transaction price. Agreements with variable consideration can still be considered contracts. The new standard provides guidance for allocating variable consideration. This guidance is outlined within step three of the model "determine the transaction price".

- The contract with the customer must have commercial substance. This requirement is designed to prevent exaggeration of revenue by the parties transferring goods or services back and forth to each other. Commercial substance exists if an entity expects the likelihood, timing, or quantity of cash received to change because of the contract. Contracts lacking commercial substance are not accounted for under the revenue recognition standard.

- The seller must be able to determine whether it is probable that the entity will collect the consideration to which it will be entitled. To make this assessment, the entity should consider the financial capacity and intent of its customer. The seller must determine the transaction price, including any price concessions, before assessing collectability.

Identifying the contract is an important first step in applying the standard and may require significant subjective judgment. If a contract is not legally enforceable or does not meet the additional requirements, then revenue recognition must be delayed. Once a contract is identified, the entity will proceed with the remaining steps in the standard.

¶ 209 STEP TWO: IDENTIFY THE PERFORMANCE OBLIGATIONS

A performance obligation is a promise to transfer a good or service. Performance obligations can be explicitly stated in the contract or implied by customary business practices or published policies outside of the contract. Activities are not considered performance obligations unless those activities transfer a good or service to a customer. Some industries have more difficulty with this step than others. For example, the insurance, software, and oil and gas industries often struggle with identifying what the right performance obligations are.

> **EXAMPLE:** Administrative tasks may not constitute a performance obligation because no good or service is transferred to the customer.

A contract may consist of one or multiple performance obligations. To determine the number of performance obligations, the entity must evaluate the concept of distinct goods and services. Distinct goods and services can give rise to multiple performance obligations. Whether goods or services are distinct or are part of a series of distinct goods or services that are substantially the same and have the same pattern of transfer to the customer can impact the number of performance obligations identified. If a good or service is not distinct, it should be combined with other goods or services until a bundle of goods or services are distinct.

Two criteria must be met for a good or service to be considered distinct:

- **The good or service is capable of being distinct.** A customer can benefit from the good or service either on its own or together with readily available resources. A good indicator is if the entity regularly sells the good or service separately.

- **The good or service is distinct within the context of the contract.** Consider whether the goods or services are separately identifiable from other promised goods or services in the contract. This concept is known as "distinct within the context of the contract".

Several conditions result in a good or service not being distinct:

- If it is bundled with other goods and services
- If the services are highly interrelated
- If the goods or services are significantly modified or customized.

Other considerations related to distinct goods and services involve the need for the entity to determine whether the nature of the contract is to transfer each good or service individually or, instead, as a combined output to the customer. ASC 606 provides a list of potential factors that would indicate that a promised good or service is separately identifiable resulting in there being one single performance obligation.

- **Significant integration service.** This factor considers whether the vendor is providing a significant service of combining promised goods or services into a combined output. If this is the case, the individual goods or services of a contract are not distinct because they represent inputs to a combined output contracted by the customer.

- **Significant modification or customization.** This factor considers whether goods or services in a contract significantly change other goods or services, which may indicate that the entity is not providing a distinct promise.

- **Highly interdependent or interrelated.** This factor considers whether goods or services significantly affect each other in such a way that the entity could not transfer these goods or services independently.

Revenue must be allocated to performance obligations and should be recognized when the goods or services are transferred to the customer. This occurs when the customer has control of the asset or use of the service. Performance obligations can be satisfied, and revenue recognized, over time or at a point in time. The principal objective is to recognize revenue in a pattern commensurate with the transfer of control of the good or service to the customer.

The method chosen to measure progress of transfer should be consistently applied to similar performance obligations and circumstances. There are two acceptable methods for measuring progress: the input method and the output method:

- **Input method.** Revenue recognition is based on the entity's effort to satisfy the performance obligation relative to the total expected effort. Examples include resources consumed, labor hours expended, costs incurred, time elapsed, or machine hours used. If a performance obligation is not satisfied over time, the obligation and revenue recognized should be considered satisfied at a point in time when control is transferred.

- **Output method.** Revenue recognition is based on the value transferred to the customer relative to the remaining value to be transferred. Examples include surveys of performance completed to date, appraisals of results achieved, milestones reached, time elapsed, and units produced or units delivered. Output methods should not be used if they do not faithfully depict the entity's performance.

  EXAMPLE: An output method based on units delivered does not faithfully depict an entity's performance if significant work-in-process exists and is not captured in the measurement method. To illustrate, suppose AAA Construction Company is going to build a new facility and buys all the materials and equipment needed for the project upfront. AAA bought the items but hasn't built anything yet. The company cannot recognize revenue because it has not yet faithfully performed the performance obligations.

STUDY QUESTIONS

1. Which of the following identifies the first step in the new revenue recognition model?

    a. Identify performance obligations in the contract.

    b. Determine the transaction price.

    c. Identify the contract(s) with a customer.

    d. Allocate the transaction price to the performance obligations in the contract.

2. Which of the following identifies the core principle of the new revenue recognition standard?

    a. Recognize revenue to depict the transfer of promised goods or services to customers in an amount reflecting the consideration to which the entity expects to be entitled in exchange for those goods or services.

    b. Ensure strong evaluation of information systems needed to adopt the standard.

    c. Develop internal and external communication plans so interested parties can understand trends.

    d. The seller must determine the transaction price, including any price concessions, before assessing collectability.

3. Which of the following identifies an impact from the new revenue recognition guidance?

    a. It involves the use of a four-step model for recognizing revenue.

    b. It provides consistent principles for recognizing revenue regardless of industry or geography.

    c. There are numerous requirements for various industries for recognizing revenue.

    d. It includes a dual model to consider variable consideration including rebates, discounts, bonuses, right of return, etc.

¶ 210 STEP THREE: DETERMINE THE TRANSACTION PRICE

The third step in the revenue recognition model is to determine the transaction price. The transaction price is the amount of consideration the entity expects to be entitled to in exchange for transferring promised goods or services. For complex contracts, such as those with variable consideration, this step can be difficult.

Consideration is variable any time it is contingent upon the occurrence or nonoccurrence of a future event. It can vary due to many reasons (discounts, rebates, refunds, credits, price concessions, incentives, performance bonuses, penalties, and right or return) and can be explicit or implicit within the contract. Under legacy GAAP, most variable revenue could not be recognized until the contingency was resolved. Under the updated standard, if a contract includes variable consideration, the entity should estimate how much consideration it will receive in order to determine how and when to recognize the variable consideration.

There are two acceptable methods for estimating variable consideration:

- **Expected value method.** This method takes the sum of the probability weighted amounts for the range of possible contract outcome.

- **Most likely amount method.** This method considers the single most likely contract outcome.

The objective is to best predict the amount of consideration to which the entity will ultimately be entitled. The expected value method is the best choice when there is a large number of contracts with similar characteristics or a contract's outcome has many possible outcomes. The most likely amount method is the best option when a contract has only two possible outcomes.

Variable consideration is included in the transaction price only to the extent it is probable that a significant reversal of cumulative revenue recognized will not occur. Factors to consider when examining this probability include the following:

- Consideration is highly susceptible to factors outside an entity's control.

- Resolution of the variable consideration will not occur for a long period of time.

- The entity has limited experience with similar contracts.

- The entity has a history of offering a broad range of price concessions.

- The contract has a broad range of possible outcomes.

Other significant factors that may impact the transaction price include:

- Refund liabilities

- Existence of a significant financing component in the contract

- Consideration payable to a customer

- Sales-based or usage-based royalty promised in exchange for a license of intellectual property

¶ 211   STEP FOUR: ALLOCATE THE TRANSACTION PRICE TO THE PERFORMANCE OBLIGATIONS

Once steps one through three are completed, an entity has identified the contract and performance obligations and determined the transaction price. The next step is to allocate the transaction price to the performance obligation. Revenue is allocated to performance obligation(s) and recognized when the goods or services are transferred to the customer. This occurs when the customer has control of the asset or use of the service. *Control* means the ability to direct the use of and obtain substantially all of the benefits from the asset or service.

The transaction price should be allocated to the performance obligations based on the relative stand-alone selling price, which is the price at which the entity would sell a good or service separately to a customer.

In determining stand-alone selling price, the best evidence to use is the observable price of a good or service when the entity sells it separately in similar circumstances. If no directly observable evidence exists, the entity must make a best estimate by maximizing the use of observable inputs. The method used should be consistently applied and include all reasonably available information. Potential estimation methods for determining stand-alone selling price include the following:

- **Adjusted market assessment.** This method requires estimation of the price a customer would pay for the good or service in the market.

- **Expected cost plus a margin.** This method estimates the expected cost to satisfy the performance obligations and then add an appropriate margin.

- **Residual.** This method estimates "the leftover price" after all observable stand-alone selling prices of other goods or services are met.

Once determined, allocation of the amount of consideration that is expected can be made to each performance obligation as it occurs.

¶ 212 STEP FIVE: RECOGNIZE REVENUE WHEN EACH PERFORMANCE OBLIGATION IS SATISFIED

This final step of the model is accomplished when the customer obtains control of the good or service. As mentioned previously, *control* means the ability to direct the use of and obtain substantially all of the benefits from the asset or service. Following are indicators of control:

- The entity has a right to payment. It has completed everything it said it would complete in the contract.

- The customer has legal title to the asset. This means the entity has transferred the title to the customer.

- The entity has transferred physical possession of the asset.

- The customer has the significant risks and rewards of ownership of the asset.

- The customer has accepted the asset.

¶ 213 KEY AREAS TO ADDRESS

Entities need to be cognizant of this five-step model for revenue recognition under the updated standard and keep in mind that it is not a "one size fits all" approach. Accounting for revenue is one of the most challenging aspects of finance and accounting, as well as one of the leading causes of restatements. Companies must specifically address some key areas as they continue to transition to the updated standard.

Because the standard relies more heavily on estimates and judgments, it requires additional data gathering and reporting, including extensive disclosures—not only about the data used, but also about the judgments that were applied when producing the estimates. The following sections discuss key areas organizations must address while implementing the new standard.

Resources and Staffing

Companies must ensure they have the proper resources, time, and knowledge to transition processes to the updated standard. Significant effort will be needed to execute the five-step model thoroughly. Many companies, especially those heavily burdened with contracts, have sought help from consultants to properly execute the five steps and evaluate all the elements.

Implementation will likely require extensive training for anyone involved in negotiating and reviewing customer contracts. This might include training for company attorneys, the purchasing department, and the accounting department. In addition, new systems and controls may need to be implemented.

Systems

Compliance with the standard may require data that is not currently being collected, aggregated, or reported. Many information technology (IT) systems do not capture and track the start and end dates for contracts, which is now required. Plus, many data elements in contracts are text fields, which make it difficult for companies to extract the specific information needed to automate certain revenue recognition processes.

Designing, developing, and testing necessary system modifications will also be a significant effort. These might include modifications to how a company executes its contracting process, how it recognizes revenue, and how that is accounted for within its finance and accounting departments.

Contracts

Contracts must be analyzed to determine if there are cases where the current terms are likely to have an undesirable impact on revenue when the updated standard is applied. The company may choose to revise its contracts to avoid undesirable impacts.

The updated revenue recognition standard assumes customer contracts will contain certain elements (provisions for termination, pricing, enforcement, etc.) that may not be present in a company's existing contracts. For that reason, a company's legal department may need to adjust the company's typical contract terms. There are two methods for disclosing contracts, the full retrospective method and the modified retrospective method.

- The full retrospective method shows financial results for the current year and two prior years presented using the updated standard.

- Under the modified retrospective method, only the current year is presented using the new standard. The two prior years are presented using the old standard accompanied by disclosures explaining how to compare the new with the old.

¶ 214 INDUSTRY IMPACT

The revised revenue recognition standard will have a significant impact on some entities but less of an effect on others. The following sections briefly review the impacts on various industries.

> **NOTE:** This list is not all-inclusive by industry or within industry. The examples are provided to give readers a sense of the scope of the new standard.

Automotive Industry

To apply the updated revenue recognition standard, original equipment manufacturers (OEMs) must evaluate the manner in which they evaluate incentives. Automotive parts suppliers must change the way they evaluate long-term supply contracts. Both entities may identify separate performance obligations under the new standard where today they do not.

Auto dealers will see impact in the following areas:

- Cash incentives
- Product or service incentives
- Extended warranty
- Vehicle leasing

In general, auto dealers will need to work through the five-step model to determine if any of the above are considered separate contracts or separate performance obligations.

Construction Industry

Construction contracts are typically long-term, with two methods for revenue recognition: percentage of completion and completed contract. Under the updated standard, the percentage-of-completion method must be used instead of the completed contract method when certain criteria are met. The completed contract method will be used in rare circumstances. In addition, criteria are set forth for combining and segmenting contracts.

Note that GAAP is not imposed on government contractors. In general, the concepts applied to construction contractors may be applied here. This may impact the methods used to recognize revenue in line with the cost accounting standards.

Biotech Industry

Companies in the biotech industry typically have complex arrangements with multiple promised goods or services (e.g., medical devices combined with installation services and a maintenance agreement). This area will require careful consideration to determine whether there are separate performance obligations. Life sciences entities may find it challenging to determine whether their collaboration agreements are in the scope of the updated standard.

Identifying the customer can be difficult for biotech companies, especially when multiple parties are involved. Evaluation may require significant judgment, and the new guidance does not provide any additional considerations in this area.

Hospital Industry

At the highest level, the new standard requires hospitals to recognize revenue:

- When promised goods or services are provided to patients
- In the amount of consideration the hospital expects to receive

Before applying the standard's model to a contract, it must be probable that the hospital will collect substantially all consideration to which it is entitled. A hospital may make this determination based on past experiences with either a specific patient or a class of similar patients—the latter of which is known as the portfolio approach. If the collectability threshold is not met, a patient contract does not exist within the scope of the standard.

> **EXAMPLE:** An uninsured patient goes to the emergency room, and the hospital attempts to assist the patient in qualifying for Medicaid. The hospital must determine the patient's ultimate payer class (Medicaid or self-pay) to be within the scope of the standard. If the payer class cannot be determined, the contract only falls within the scope of the standard once the payer class is confirmed.

Software Industry

The biggest impact to this industry will be ensuring that pervasive evidence of an arrangement exists. Before revenue can be recognized:

- There must be a valid contract with a customer.
- The software must exist and be delivered; it cannot be in the development stage.
- The price must be independent of the quantity of users.
- There must be no concessions that make the price uncollectible.

Oil and Gas Industry

To adopt the new revenue recognition model, oil and gas entities will need to change the way they evaluate many of their transactions. They must carefully evaluate how the new revenue recognition standard may affect specific contracts upstream, midstream, and downstream, as well as the financial reporting process overall.

Properly identifying the performance obligations in these contracts may be complex but will be critical because these determinations will drive the pattern of revenue recognition. Oil and gas entities may need to use significant judgment to evaluate who has mineral rights versus who has surface rights to determine the individual performance obligations within the contract.

¶ 215 SUMMARY

Each industry may be impacted differently by the new revenue recognition standard. Entities should follow the AICPA industry guides and task forces to ensure they are taking the proper steps for compliance for their industry.

This chapter was designed to provide the "technical" applications of the updated revenue recognition standards and outline the steps within the new model. Some examples and considerations were included within each step. In addition, the text compared and contrasted the new model to the previous model.

Overall, the expectation is the updated standard will provide a more consistent approach to revenue recognition. Compliance with the standard will take diligence by accounting professionals.

STUDY QUESTIONS

4. With respect to identifying a contract with a customer, each of the following are common-law elements of a contract, *except:*

    a. Equitability

    b. Agreement

    c. Consideration

    d. Capacity

5. Which of the following identifies a type of output method as it relates to performance obligations?

    a. Resources consumed

    b. Labor hours expended

    c. Machine hours used

    d. Units produced

6. The largest impact to the _____ industry will be ensuring pervasive evidence of an arrangement exists.

    a. Automotive

    b. Construction

    c. Software

    d. Biotech

CPE NOTE: When you have completed your study and review of chapters 1 and 2, which comprise Module 1, you may wish to take the Final Exam for this Module. Go to **cchcpelink.com/printcpe** to take this Final Exam online.

MODULE 2: TOP AUDITING ISSUES— CHAPTER 3: New Auditing Standards in SASs Nos. 134–141

¶ 301 WELCOME

This chapter provides a brief review of the background to the changes in auditing standards and then outlines specific changes to Generally Accepted Auditing Standards (GAAS) from the following Statements on Auditing Standards (SAS) released by the AICPA Auditing Standards Board (ASB): SAS No. 134, *Auditor Reporting and Amendments, Including Amendments Addressing Disclosures in the Audit of Financial Statements*; SAS No. 135, *Omnibus Statement on Auditing Standards—2019*; SAS No. 136, *Forming an Opinion and Reporting on Financial Statements of Employee Benefit Plans Subject to ERISA*; SAS No. 137, *The Auditor's Responsibilities Relating to Other Information Included in Annual Reports*; SAS No. 138, *Amendments to the Description of the Concept of Materiality*, and SSAE No. 20 of the same title; SAS No. 139, *Amendments to AU-C Sections 800, 805, and 810 to Incorporate Auditor Reporting Changes from SAS No. 134*; SAS No. 140, *Amendments to AU-C Sections 725, 730, 930, 935, and 940 to Incorporate Auditor Reporting Changes from SAS Nos. 134 and 137*; and SAS No. 141, *Amendment to the Effective Dates of SAS Nos. 134–140*. The chapter also reviews illustrations of audit reports with new changes and updates on other important issues.

¶ 302 LEARNING OBJECTIVES

Upon completion of this chapter, you will be able to:

- Identify how to implement the new and extensive audit report format, disclosures, and procedures
- Differentiate AU-C sections and how they apply to the auditor's responsibilities
- Recognize when the updates to Statements on Auditing Standards (SAS) sections by the Accounting Standards Board (ASB) are effective
- Identify how AU-C sections apply to financial statements
- Differentiate the "Opinion" section of the auditor's report and what is included
- Identify where the auditor's report should name the city and state
- Describe what should be exercised and maintained by the auditor in accordance with GAAS

¶ 303 INTRODUCTION

SAS No. 134, *Auditor Reporting and Amendments, Including Amendments Addressing Disclosures in the Audit of Financial Statements*, makes major changes to the form and content of the non-issuing (nonpublic) auditor's report for non-issuing entities. This chapter will address specific changes to the standards for the auditor's responsibility in forming an opinion. Further, changes have been made so users will benefit by having the auditor's report format changed, and the chapter will address the format change and the content changes that were made for added transparency purposes for the auditor's opinion and auditor and management responsibilities.

¶ 304 CHANGES FROM REVISIONS TO AUDITING STANDARDS

The call for changes to the auditor reporting model in the United States and other jurisdictions around the world came from users of the financial statements and the auditor's report, who wanted more information about significant aspects of an audit. The financial crisis of 2007–2008 also played a role in bringing about changes.

The AICPA's Auditing Standards Board (ASB), which issues the auditing standards for nonpublic entities, monitored developments related to the auditor reporting model in the United States and around the world. In particular, the ASB followed auditor reporting projects of the International Auditing and Assurance Standards Board (IAASB) and the Public Company Accounting Oversight Board (PCAOB), which sets standards in the United States for publicly held companies.

The ASB Auditor Reporting Task Force was formed to consider the implications of these projects on auditor's reports issued for audits of non-issuers. Investors and other users of financial statements, as well as regulators, corporate governance organizations, auditors, and others, provided their input in response to proposals and requests for public comment from these standard-setters relating to changes to the auditor's report.

Several key themes emerged from that process. The users—the individuals actually looking at the financial statements issued by auditor—indicated they continued to value the pass-fail nature of the auditor's opinion but that the rest of the auditor's report was boilerplate in nature and did not offer much transparency into the audit. Some users wanted more and better information about audit areas that posed higher risks of material misstatement or involved significant management and auditor judgment, or about areas related to significant events or transactions.

In an effort to address the expectations gap, users and other stakeholders also expressed a desire to expand the audit report's description of management's responsibilities for the preparation of the financial statements, and of the auditor's responsibilities for the audit of the financial statements.

There were some considerations for other projects as well. The ASB also took into account the revisions to the auditor's report resulting from the IAASB and PCAOB projects in developing the GAAS changes outlined in its exposure draft. According to the ASB, the changes will boost the informational value and relevance of the auditor's report for users.

The overall theme of some of the auditor reporting models today is convergence—especially among the ASB, IAASB, and PCAOB standards. The ASB's strategy is to converge its standards with the IAASB's. To that end, the ASB develops its standards based on the corresponding International Standards on Auditing (ISAs). When making its proposed revisions to the accompanying proposed SASs, the ASB used ISAs 700 (Revised), 701, 705 (Revised), and 706 (Revised) as the base standards.

Although the ASB has made certain changes to language, terms, and phrases that make the standards appropriate for the U.S. environment, it believes that such changes do not create substantive differences in application. To get a better idea of what changes were made, let's first look at the PCAOB auditor reporting model.

¶ 305 PCAOB AUDITOR REPORTING MODEL

On June 1, 2017, the PCAOB adopted a new auditing standard, AS 3101, *The Auditor's Report on an Audit of Financial Statements When the Auditor Expresses an Unqualified Opinion* (hereinafter referred to as the new PCAOB standard), and related amendments to its existing auditing standards.

The new PCAOB standard, which retains the pass-or-fail nature of the auditor's opinion, is intended to enhance the relevance and usefulness of the auditor's report by providing additional and important information to investors. The new PCAOB standard resembles the IAASB's changes to the auditor's report in many ways, including the following:

- Both the PCAOB and IAASB require the "Opinion" section to be presented first in the auditor's report, with the "Basis for Opinion" section next.
- Both require a more explicit reference to independence in the "Basis for Opinion" section. There are also some ethical considerations in that section.

There are some differences between the two, however, regarding the form of the auditor's report. The IAASB requires a more extensive description of the responsibilities of management and the auditor for the preparation and audit of the financial statements, respectively.

An important change in the new PCAOB standard is the requirement of a discussion of critical audit matters (CAMs) in the auditor's report for audits conducted in accordance with the PCAOB standards. However, certain types of entities are specifically scoped out of the CAM requirement. The new PCAOB standard defines a CAM as any matter arising from the audit of the financial statements that was communicated or was required to be communicated to the audit committee, and that relates to accounts or disclosures that are material to the financial statements and involved especially challenging, subjective, or complex auditor judgment. Meeting this requirement will obviously involve a bit more documentation on the auditor's part.

Regarding the IAASB's approach to determining key audit matters (KAMs), and auditor reporting models in other jurisdictions that require similar matters to be discussed in the auditor's report, the PCAOB stated that "although the processes of identifying these matters vary across jurisdictions, there are commonalities in the underlying criteria regarding matters to be communicated and the communication requirements, such that expanded auditor reporting could result in the communication of many of the same matters under the various approaches."

The requirements in the new PCAOB standard are quite similar to those in the PCAOB's May 2016 re-proposal of the auditor reporting standard for public comment. For entities that are either publicly held or are planning to go public, these requirements could be critical. The ASB considered the requirements in the PCAOB re-proposal in the development of the proposed SASs and related amendments.

> **COMMENT:** Note that while the ASB's primary focus is on convergence with the ISAs, it does want to converge with the PCAOB standards as well.

Effective dates. For all elements of the PCAOB auditor's report other than CAMs, the effective date for PCAOB audits is for fiscal years ending on or after December 15, 2017. The effective date for CAMs is for fiscal years ending on or after June 30, 2019, for audits of large accelerated filers, and for fiscal years ending on or after December 15, 2020, for audits of all other companies to which the new PCAOB standard applies. The Securities and Exchange Commission (SEC) approved the final standard and amendments on October 23, 2017.

STUDY QUESTIONS

1. Statements on Auditing Standards (SAS) are promulgated by which AICPA committee?

    a. Accounting and Review Services Committee

    b. Assurance Services Executive Committee

    c. Auditing Standards Board

    d. Center for Audit Quality

2. What are matters arising from the audit of the financial statements that was communicated to the audit committee, and that relate to accounts or disclosures that are material and involved especially challenging, subjective, or complex auditor judgment?

    a. Reportable events

    b. Key audit matters

    c. Critical audit matters

    d. Control deficiency

¶ 306 SUMMARY OF SIGNIFICANT CHANGES

The following list summarizes what the ASB believes are the most significant changes in the proposed SAS from AU-C Section 700. "AU" is the auditing standards codification that comes from the ASB on U.S. GAAS, and Section 700 is part of that. The "-C" relates to clarity; it means the clarity process was used. In its Clarity Project, the ASB took on the task of rewriting and redrafting all audit positions. With the release of SSAE 18, the Clarity Project was closed.

AU-C Section 700:

- Requires the "Opinion" section to be presented first in the auditor's report, followed by the "Basis for Opinion" section, unless laws or regulation state otherwise.

- Requires the "Basis for Opinion" section of the auditor's report to include an affirmative statement about the auditor's independence and fulfillment of the auditor's other ethical responsibilities in accordance with relevant ethical requirements relating to the audit.

    COMMENT: The "auditor's other ethical responsibilities in accordance with relevant ethical requirements" mentioned above are outlined in the AICPA Code of Professional Conduct, which was last revised in 2017. Firms in a peer review program must have a quality control document that sets out the firm's policies and procedures that will be used to perform the attest functions on its engagements. These include any relevant checklists, forms, and standards. Firms that have not updated their quality control policies and procedures manual under Statement on Quality Control Standards No. 8 should update them immediately to comply with the revised Code of Professional Conduct.

- Requires the auditor to report in accordance with proposed amendments to AU-C Section 570, *The Auditor's Consideration of an Entity's Ability to Continue as a Going Concern.*

    COMMENT: This represents a significant change. Management now has the responsibility to make the assessment of going concern. The auditor's must evaluate that assessment to make sure that it is correct and appropriate, and that management and the auditor agree.

- Does not require communication of KAMs for audits of non-issuers. However, if the terms of the audit engagement include reporting KAMs, the auditor would be required to communicate KAMs in accordance with proposed SAS, *Communicating Key Audit Matters in the Independent Auditor's Report*.

- Requires the auditor to report in accordance with SAS No. 137, *The Auditor's Responsibilities Relating to Other Information Included in Annual Reports*

- Expands the description of management's responsibilities for the preparation and fair presentation of the financial statements, and includes a requirement to identify those responsible for the oversight of the financial reporting process when they differ from those responsible for the preparation of the financial statements.

- Expands the description of the responsibilities of the auditor and key features of an audit.

¶ 307 NEW STANDARD: SAS NO. 134

SAS No. 134 was issued by the ASB in May 2019. It represents major changes in auditor reporting that have not been seen in many years. The specific changes by section are as follows:

- AICPA, Professional Standards, AU-C Section 701, supersedes the following sections of SAS No. 122, *Statements on Auditing Standards: Clarification and Recodification*, as amended:

  — Section 700, *Forming an Opinion and Reporting on Financial Statements* (AICPA, Professional Standards, AU-C Section 700)

  — Section 705, *Modifications to the Opinion in the Independent Auditor's Report* (AICPA, Professional Standards, AU-C Section 705)

  — Section 706, *Emphasis-of-Matter Paragraphs and Other-Matter Paragraphs in the Independent Auditor's Report* (AICPA, Professional Standards, AU-C Section 706)

- It amends the following sections of SAS No. 122, as amended:

  — Section 200, *Overall Objectives of the Independent Auditor and the Conduct of an Audit in Accordance With Generally Accepted Auditing Standards* (AICPA, Professional Standards, AU-C Section 200)

  — Section 210, *Terms of Engagement* (AICPA, Professional Standards, AU-C Section 210)

  — Section 220, *Quality Control for an Engagement Conducted in Accordance With Generally Accepted Auditing Standards* (AICPA, Professional Standards, AU-C Section 220)

  — Section 230, *Audit Documentation* (AICPA, Professional Standards, AU-C Section 230)

  — Section 240, *Consideration of Fraud in a Financial Statement Audit* (AICPA, Professional Standards, AU-C Section 240)

  — Section 260, *The Auditor's Communication With Those Charged With Governance* (AICPA, Professional Standards, AU-C Section 260)

  — Section 300, *Planning an Audit* (AICPA, Professional Standards, AU-C Section 300)

- — Section 315, *Understanding the Entity and Its Environment and Assessing the Risks of Material Misstatement* (AICPA, Professional Standards, AU-C Section 315)

- — Section 320, *Materiality in Planning and Performing an Audit* (AICPA, Professional Standards, AU-C Section 320)

- — Section 330, *Performing Audit Procedures in Response to Assessed Risks and Evaluating the Audit Evidence Obtained* (AICPA, Professional Standards, AU-C Section 330)

- — Section 450, *Evaluation of Misstatements Identified During the Audit* (AICPA, Professional Standards, AU-C Section 450)

- — Section 510, *Opening Balances—Initial Audit Engagements, Including Reaudit Engagements* (AICPA, Professional Standards, AU-C Section 510)

- — Section 540, *Auditing Accounting Estimates, Including Fair Value Accounting Estimates, and Related Disclosures* (AICPA, Professional Standards, AU-C Section 540)

- — Section 600, *Special Considerations—Audits of Group Financial Statements [Including the Work of Component Auditors], as amended* (AICPA, Professional Standards, AU-C Section 600)

- — Section 910, *Financial Statements Prepared in Accordance With a Financial Reporting Framework Generally Accepted in Another Country*

- • It also amends SAS No. 132, *The Auditor's Consideration of an Entity's Ability to Continue as a Going Concern* (AICPA, Professional Standards, AU-C Section 570).

Effective date. This section was originally effective for audits of financial statements for periods ending on or after December 15, 2020, and early implementation was not permitted. See SAS No. 141 for changes to the effective date and early implementation. SAS No. 141 changed the effective date to periods ending on or after December 15, 2021, and also allows for early implementation of the changes.

¶ 308 AU-C SECTION 700, FORMING AN OPINION AND REPORTING ON FINANCIAL STATEMENTS

Scope

This section discusses the auditor's responsibility to form an opinion as well as the form and content of the auditor's report issued as a result of a financial statements audit. It applies to an audit of a complete set of general-purpose financial statements and is written in that context. However, this section does not apply when the auditor is forming an opinion and reporting on financial statements of employee benefit plans that are subject to the Employee Retirement Income Security Act of 1974 (ERISA). In that case, SAS No. 136, *Forming an Opinion and Reporting on Financial Statements of Employee Benefit Plans Subject to ERISA*, which was issued in July 2019, applies. Therefore, auditors working on engagements involving a financial statement of an employee benefit plan subject to ERISA should refer to SAS No. 136 rather than SAS No. 134.

- • AU-C Section 705 discusses how the form and content of the auditor's report are affected when the auditor (1) expresses a modified opinion (also called a *qualified opinion, adverse opinion,* or *disclaimer of opinion*) or (2) includes an emphasis-of-matter paragraph or other-matter paragraph in the auditor's report. This section does not require the communication of KAMs. Section 701, *Com-*

municating Key Audit Matters in the Independent Auditor's Report, discusses the auditor's responsibility to communicate KAMs when the auditor is engaged to do so.

- AU-C Section 800 addresses special considerations when financial statements are prepared in accordance with a special purpose framework.

- AU-C Section 805 addresses special considerations relevant to an audit of a single financial statement or of a specific element, account, or item of a financial statement.

The requirements of this section promote consistency and comparability in auditor reporting. Consistency in the auditor's report, when the audit has been conducted in accordance with GAAS, promotes credibility in the marketplace by making audits that have been conducted in accordance with recognized standards more easily identifiable. Consistency also helps promote users' understanding and identification of unusual circumstances when they occur.

Objectives

The auditor's objectives are to (1) form an opinion on the financial statements based on an evaluation of the audit evidence, including evidence about comparative financial statements or comparative financial information; and (2) clearly express, in a written report, an opinion on the financial statements.

Definitions

SAS No. 134 provides the following definitions:

- **Comparative financial statements:** A complete set of financial statements for one or more prior periods included for comparison with the financial statements of the current period.

- **Comparative information:** Prior period information presented for purposes of comparison with current period amounts or disclosures that is not in the form of a complete set of financial statements. Comparative information includes prior period information presented as condensed financial statements or summarized financial information.

- **Condensed financial statements:** Historical financial information that is presented in less detail than a complete set of financial statements, in accordance with an appropriate financial reporting framework. Condensed financial statements may be separately presented as unaudited financial information or may be presented as comparative information.

- **General purpose financial statements:** Financial statements prepared in accordance with a general purpose framework.

- **General purpose framework:** A financial reporting framework designed to meet the common financial information needs of a wide range of users.

- **Unmodified opinion:** The opinion expressed by the auditor when the auditor concludes that the financial statements are presented fairly, in all material respects, in accordance with the applicable financial reporting framework.

As used in this section, the term *financial statements* refers to a complete set of general purpose financial statements. The requirements of the applicable financial reporting framework determine the presentation, structure, and content of the financial statements and what constitutes a complete set of financial statements.

¶308

Auditor's Report

First, and most important, the auditor's report should be in writing. This means the auditor can hand-write the report, type it, or use word processing equipment to create it. It should be in a written format.

The auditor's report for audits conducted in accordance with GAAS should have a title that clearly indicates that it is the report of an independent auditor, and the report should be addressed as appropriate based on the circumstances of the engagement. A good title is "Independent Audit." The auditor's report must be addressed like a report, not a letter, so it should not include an inside address such as Jane Doe, President of ABC Company, 123 Elm Street, Anywhere USA. Although there is no real requirement, it is good practice to simply address the report to the board of directors, the audit committee, the president, or other appropriate addressee, and include the city and state. The critical piece is that it should have a title that clearly indicates it is the report of an independent auditor.

The first section of the auditor's report should include the auditor's opinion and should have the heading "Opinion." This a major change from previous guidance. The Opinion section should:

- Identify the entity whose financial statements have been audited
- State that the financial statements have been audited
- Identify the title of each statement that the financial statements comprise
- Refer to the notes
- Specify the dates of or periods covered by each financial statement that the financial statements comprise

If an auditor expresses an unmodified opinion on the financial statements, the auditor's opinion should state that, in the auditor's opinion, the accompanying financial statements present fairly, in all material respects, [XX] in accordance with [the applicable financial reporting framework and its origin].

The "Basis for Opinion" section comes immediately after the "Opinion" section and should:

- State that the audit was conducted in accordance with GAAS and identify the United States as the country of origin of GAAS. (Because many other countries have their own standards, it is important to clarify that the United States is the country of origin.)
- Refer to the section of the auditor's report that describes the auditor's responsibilities under GAAS.
- Provide a statement that the auditor is required to be independent of the entity and meet the relevant ethical requirements relating to the audit.
- State whether the auditor believes that the audit evidence obtained is sufficient and appropriate to provide a basis for the auditor's opinion.

If applicable, the auditor should report in accordance with AU-C Section 570, *The Auditor's Consideration of an Entity's Ability to Continue as a Going Concern*. The auditor should state that management has concluded that the entity is a going concern entity. This means the financial statements were prepared in accordance with a going concern basis of accounting.

Key Audit Matters

When engaged to communicate KAMs, the auditor should do so in accordance with Section 701 of this SAS.

Management's Responsibilities for the Financial Statements

A section with the heading "Responsibilities of Management for the Financial Statements" should be included in the auditor's report. This section should describe management's responsibility for:

- The preparation and fair presentation of the financial statements in accordance with the applicable financial reporting framework, and for the design, implementation, and maintenance of internal control relevant to the preparation and fair presentation of financial statements that are free from material misstatement, whether due to fraud or error

- When required by the applicable financial reporting framework, the evaluation of whether conditions or events exist that raise substantial doubt about the entity's ability to continue as a going concern (for the period set by the applicable financial reporting framework, as applicable).

The description of management's responsibility for the financial statements should not refer to a separate statement by management about its responsibilities. This is true even if that type of statement is included in a document that contains the auditor's report.

Auditor's Responsibilities for the Audit of the Financial Statements

The auditor's responsibilities should be outlined in a section titled "Auditor's Responsibilities for the Audit of the Financial Statements." This section should state the following:

- That the auditor's objectives are to obtain reasonable assurance about whether the financial statements as a whole are free from material misstatement, whether due to fraud or error, and issue an auditor's report that includes the auditor's opinion.

- That reasonable assurance is a high level of assurance but not absolute assurance, and therefore it is not a guarantee that an audit conducted in accordance with GAAS will always detect a material misstatement that exists.

- That the risk of not detecting a material misstatement resulting from fraud is higher than for one resulting from error, because fraud may involve collusion, forgery, intentional omissions, misrepresentations, or the override of internal control.

- That misstatements are considered material if, individually or in the aggregate, they could reasonably be expected to influence economic decisions users make based on these financial statements.

This section should also state that, in performing an audit in accordance with GAAS, the auditor is responsible for:

- Exercising professional judgment and maintaining professional skepticism throughout the audit

  COMMENT: Note that the PCAOB identified the failure to maintain professional skepticism to identify and address the risk of material misstatement of the financial statements, whether due to fraud or error, as one of the top problematic issues in audits.

- Identifying and assessing the risks of material misstatement of the financial statements, whether resulting from fraud or error, and designing and performing audit procedures that respond to those risks.

- Obtaining an understanding of the entity's internal control relevant to the audit in order to design appropriate audit procedures, but not for the purpose of expressing an opinion on the effectiveness of the entity's internal control. Accordingly, no such opinion is expressed.

— In situations where the auditor also has a responsibility to express an opinion on the effectiveness of internal control in conjunction with the audit of the financial statements, the auditor should omit the following: "but not for the purpose of expressing an opinion on the effectiveness of the entity's internal control. Accordingly, no such opinion is expressed."

- Evaluating the appropriateness of the accounting policies used and the reasonableness of significant accounting estimates made by management, and also evaluating the overall presentation of the financial statements.

- Concluding whether, in the auditor's judgment, conditions or events exist that raise substantial doubt about the entity's ability to continue as a going concern for a reasonable period of time.

In addition, this section of the auditor's report should note that the auditor is required to communicate with those charged with governance regarding the planned scope and timing of the audit, significant audit findings, and certain internal control–related matters that the auditor identified during the audit, among other issues.

If the auditor has other reporting responsibilities besides the responsibilities under GAAS, these should be addressed in a separate section in the auditor's report with the heading "Report on Other Legal and Regulatory Requirements" or another heading that is appropriate.

Signature, City and State, and Date

The auditor's report should include the manual or printed signature of the auditor's firm as well as the city and state where the auditor's report is issued. Even if the firm's letterhead includes the city and state, it is good practice to put the city and state in the auditor's report. This is especially important for multi-office firms whose letterhead might be silent as to the city and state of the particular office that issued the auditor's report.

The date of the auditor's report is especially important. The report should be dated no earlier than the date on which the auditor obtained sufficient appropriate audit evidence on which to base his opinion on the financial statements, including evidence that:

- All the statements and disclosures that the financial statements comprise have been prepared.

- Management has asserted that it has taken responsibility for those financial statements.

Other Matters in SAS No. 134

Specific issues include:

- Auditor's Report for Audits Conducted in Accordance With Both GAAS and Another Set of Auditing Standards

- Auditor's Report for Audits Conducted in Accordance With the Standards of the PCAOB and GAAS When the Audit Is Not Within the Jurisdiction of the PCAOB

- Comparative Financial Statements and Comparative Information

- Prior Period Financial Statements Audited by a Predecessor Auditor

- Prior Period Financial Statements Not Audited

STUDY QUESTIONS

3. A significant change to AU-C Section _____ requires the "Opinion" section to be presented first in the auditor's report, followed by the "Basis for Opinion" section, unless law or regulation prescribe otherwise.

    a. 570

    b. 700

    c. 402

    d. 303

4. AU-C 705 addresses which type of opinion in the independent auditor's report?

    a. Qualified

    b. Modified

    c. Adverse

    d. Disclaimer

¶ 309 ILLUSTRATIONS OF SPECIFIC CONSIDERATIONS

In the SAS No. 134 exhibit titled "Illustrations of Auditor's Reports on Financial Statements," the ASB provides several illustrations of auditor's reports on financial statements highlighting specific considerations related to SAS No. 134. Each illustration includes a list of the circumstances and a sample auditor's report.

The illustration topics are listed below. The reader is encouraged to access SAS No. 134 at https://www.aicpa.org/content/dam/aicpa/research/standards/auditattest/downloadabledocuments/sas-134.pdf to view the full text of the illustrations.

- Illustration 1: An Auditor's Report on Comparative Financial Statements Prepared in Accordance With Accounting Principles Generally Accepted in the United States of America

- Illustration 2: An Auditor's Report on Comparative Financial Statements Prepared in Accordance With Accounting Principles Generally Accepted in the United States of America, Including Communication of Key Audit Matters

- Illustration 3: An Auditor's Report on Financial Statements for a Single Year Prepared in Accordance With Accounting Principles Generally Accepted in the United States of America

- Illustration 4: An Auditor's Report on Comparative Financial Statements Prepared in Accordance With Accounting Principles Generally Accepted in the United States of America When the Audit Has Been Conducted in Accordance With Both Auditing Standards Generally Accepted in the United States of America and International Standards on Auditing

- Illustration 5: An Auditor's Report on Financial Statements for a Single Year Prepared in Accordance With Accounting Principles Generally Accepted in the United States of America When Comparative Summarized Financial Information Derived From Audited Financial Statements for the Prior Year Is Presented

- Illustration 6: An Auditor's Report on Financial Statements for a Single Year Prepared in Accordance With Accounting Principles Generally Accepted in the United States of America When Comparative Summarized Financial Information Derived From Unaudited Financial Statements for the Prior Year Is Presented

- Illustration 7: An Auditor's Report on Comparative Financial Statements Prepared in Accordance With Accounting Principles Generally Accepted in the United States of America When the Audit Has Been Conducted by a Registered Firm in Accordance With Both Auditing Standards Generally Accepted in the United States of America and the Auditing and Professional Practice Standards of the Public Company Accounting Oversight Board

- Illustration 8: An Auditor's Report on Comparative Financial Statements Prepared in Accordance With Accounting Principles Generally Accepted in the United States of America When the Audit Has Been Conducted by a Nonregistered Firm in Accordance With Both Auditing Standards Generally Accepted in the United States of America and the Auditing Standards of the Public Company Accounting Oversight Board

¶ 310 THE SIGNIFICANCE OF SAS NO. 141

SAS No. 141 amended the following SASs in significant ways. First, SAS No. 141 amended the effective dates of seven SASs as listed:

- SAS No. 134, *Auditor Reporting and Amendments, Including Amendments Addressing Disclosures in the Audit of Financial Statements*, as amended
- SAS No. 135, *Omnibus Statement on Auditing Standards—2019*
- SAS No. 136, *Forming an Opinion and Reporting on Financial Statements of Employee Benefit Plans Subject to ERISA*, as amended
- SAS No. 137, *The Auditor's Responsibilities Relating to Other Information Included in Annual Reports*
- SAS No. 138, *Amendments to the Description of the Concept of Materiality*
- SAS No. 139, *Amendments to AU-C Sections 800, 805, and 810 to Incorporate Auditor Reporting Changes from SAS No. 134*
- SAS No. 140, *Amendments to AU-C Sections 725, 730,930, and 940 to Incorporate Auditor Reporting Changes from SAS Nos. 134 and 137*

SAS No. 141 changed the effective dates of SAS Nos. 134–140 to periods ending after December 15, 2021. This means that periods ending December 31, 2021, would be the most dates affected. The ASB wanted to provide more time for firms to put the SASs in place because of the problems with the COVID-19 pandemic. Further, SAS Nos. 134–140 did not allow for early implementation. SAS No. 141 changes all seven of those SASs to allow early implementation if desired.

The ASB considers all seven SASs to be related because of changes in the SASs that followed SAS No. 134. Therefore, the ASB wants all of the seven SASs to be put in as connected and placed in effect concurrently. SAS No. 141 is effective on its issue date in May 2020.

STUDY QUESTIONS

5. The terms of the audit engagement reflect the description of management's responsibility for the financial statements in AU—C Section:

    a. 210

    b. 230

    c. 250

    d. 260

6. Management is responsible for the preparation of the financial statements in accordance with accounting principles generally accepted in the United States of America as promulgated by the:

    a. Public Company Accounting Oversight Board (PCAOB)

    b. Financial Accounting Standards Board (FASB)

    c. American Institute of Certified Public Accountants (AICPA)

    d. Government Accountability Office (GAO)

MODULE 2: TOP AUDITING ISSUES— CHAPTER 4: Materiality Changes

¶ 401 WELCOME

This chapter discusses the new standards from the Auditing Standards Board (ASB) that amend the description of the concept of materiality. It provides an overview of Statement on Auditing Standards (SAS) No. 138, *Amendments to the Description of the Concept of Materiality*; Statement on Standards for Attestation Engagements (SSAE) No. 20 (of the same title); and Statements on Standards for Accounting and Review Services (SSARS) 25, *Materiality in a Review of Financial Statements and Adverse Conclusions*.

This chapter also discusses SAS No. 141, *Amendments to the Effective Dates of SASs Nos. 134-140*. SAS No. 141 changes the effective dates of SASs Nos. 134-140 from periods ending on or after December 15, 2020, for one year to periods ending on or after December 15, 2021. This was done in order to provide more time to implement SASs Nos. 134-140 due to the COVID-19 pandemic.

¶ 402 LEARNING OBJECTIVES

Upon completion of this chapter, you will be able to:

- Recognize and apply the concept of materiality to financial applications
- Differentiate the nuances in the definition of materiality
- Recognize and apply the concept of materiality to audit considerations in an audit
- Understand materiality and risks
- Understand the use of materiality in attestation engagements
- Understand the effective date changes of SASs 134-140

¶ 403 INTRODUCTION

In June of 2019, the Auditing Standards Board (ASB) of the American Institute of Certified Public Accountants (AICPA) issued a Proposed Statement on Auditing Standards, *Amendments to the Description of the Concept of Materiality*, and a Proposed Statement on Standards for Attestation Engagements, *Amendments to the Description of the Concept of Materiality*. These proposals were issued in December 2019 as SAS No. 138 and SSAE No. 20 and amend the following SASs:

- SAS No. 122, *Statements on Auditing Standards: Clarification and Recodification*
- SAS No. 134, *Auditor Reporting and Amendments, Including Amendments Addressing Disclosures in the Audit of the Financial Statement*
- SAS No. 136, *Forming an Opinion and Reporting on Financial Statements of Employee Benefit Plans Subject to ERISA [AICPA, Professional Standards, AU-C sec. 703]*

The new standards apply to audits of financial statements for periods ending on or after December 15, 2021 (SAS No. 138) and practitioners' examination and review reports dated on or after December 15, 2021 (SSAE No. 20).

SAS No. 138, SSAE No. 20, and SSARS No. 25 amend various AU-C, AT-C, and AR-C sections, respectively, in AICPA Professional Standards, to make the materiality concepts discussed in AICPA Professional Standards consistent with the description of materiality used by the U.S. judicial system and with the auditing standards of the Public Company Accounting Oversight Board (PCAOB), the U.S. Securities and Exchange Commission (SEC), and the Financial and Accounting Standards Board (FASB).

The materiality concept applies in a wide variety of contexts, including accounting, reporting, business, financial, legal, risk, and more recently, environmental, social, and governance or sustainability or nonfinancial issues. The history of the concept dates back to 1867, when the English Court introduced the term *material* by referring to "relevant, not negligible fact" that emerged in the judgment of the false accounting case concerning the Central Railways of Venezuela. The English Common Law could indeed be considered as the cradle of the concept of materiality. Materiality has quickly become essential for stakeholder engagement exercises and topic mapping while appearing as a keyword in consultant pitches.

Sustainability professionals around the world scrambled to understand the term and the process, outlined by standard-setters like the Global Reporting Initiative (GRI) and the International Integrated Reporting Council (IIRC).

As a concept borrowed from the accounting and auditing domain, materiality represented the perfect idea to foster the integration of nonfinancial issues into mainstream business thinking and decision-making.

¶ 404 MATERIALITY DEFINITIONS

Many different definitions of *materiality* exist. In the context of sustainability or nonfinancial reporting, one of the Corporate Reporting Dialogue (CRD) statements of the common principles of materiality is: "Material information is that which is reasonably capable of making a difference to the proper evaluation of the issue at hand."

There are also several definitions of *materiality* or *material information* from a regulatory perspective. For example, according to the SEC, "a matter is material if there is a substantial likelihood that a reasonable person would consider it important." The SEC's stance is that it will not issue specific disclosures; rather, companies are in charge of assessing material risks.

The U.S. Supreme Court indicated that information is material if there is "a substantial likelihood that the disclosure of the omitted fact would have been viewed by the reasonable investor as having significantly altered the 'total mix' of information made available."

Standard-setting bodies also have defined the term. The International Financial Reporting Standards (IFRS) Foundation defines materiality as follows: "Information is material if omitting, misstating or obscuring it could reasonably be expected to influence the decisions that the primary users of general purpose financial statements make on the basis of those financial statements, which provide financial information about a specific reporting entity."

> **NOTE:** The existing definition of materiality in the AICPA standards is consistent with the definition used by the International Accounting Standards Board (IASB) and the International Auditing and Assurance Standards Board (IAASB).

The International Organization of Standardization Guidance on Social Responsibility (ISO 26000) offers the following definition: "An organization should review all the core subjects to identify which issues are relevant. The identification of relevant issues should be followed by an assessment of the significance of the organization's impacts. The significance of an impact should be considered with reference both to the stakeholders concerned and to the way in which the impact affects sustainable development."

The World Federation of Exchanges (WFE) Investor Group, being well represented by the World Federation of Exchanges (WFE) ESG Guidance and Metrics, suggests: "Materiality is often locally determined and different investors may have different perspectives on what they would consider to be material. As indicated above, it is clear however that investors wish to understand:

- How the firm determines materiality and who was involved in determining which issues are material;
- Which issues the firm believes are material;
- How the company has decided that these are material (process, timeframe, relevant legal framework, etc.); and
- How the identified issues are integrated into corporate strategy and what impact they could have on value creation."

The Task Force on Climate-Related Financial Disclosures, the other investor-led coalition that bridges the gap between the corporate and finance communities, says: "[Referring to] materiality as a concept designed to guide the application of professional judgement for the purpose of determining acceptable levels of information disclosure in mainstream reports and thereby informing decision-making by the users of those reports."

In the context of risk management, the "Enterprise Risk Management—Integrating with Strategy and Performance Framework" by the Committee of Sponsoring Organizations of the Treadway Commission (COSO) and World Business Council on Sustainable Development (WBCSD) define material risk as "the possibility that events will occur and affect the achievement of strategy and business objectives." Importantly, both negative effects (e.g., a reduction in revenue targets or damage to reputation) and positive impacts or opportunities (including an emerging market for new products or cost savings initiatives) are included.

Overall, these definitions provide two major perspectives:

- One is stakeholder oriented as it emphasizes the impacts an organization has on the environment and society.
- The other has a stronger focus on an organization, as it is centered on the affects the environment and society have on the organization.

Interestingly, earlier in 2019, the EU Commission released the Consultation Document on the Update of the Non-Binding Guidelines on the EU Non-Financial Reporting Directive (NFRD). It was the first policy to merge these perspectives in one. The document introduces a new definition of materiality called *double materiality*. The first perspective concerns the potential or actual impacts of climate-related risk and opportunities on the "performance, development and position" of the company (indicated as "financial materiality," with an investor type of audience). The latter refers to the "external impacts of the company's activities" (labeled as "environmental and social materiality," whose audience consists of consumers, civil society, employees, and also investors).

SAS No. 138 and SSAE No. 20 align the materiality concepts discussed in AICPA Professional Standards with the definition of materiality used by the U.S. judicial system, and the auditing standards of the PCAOB, SEC, and FASB. According to the ASB's new definition, financial reporting frameworks generally explain that "misstatements, including omissions, are considered to be material if there is a substantial likelihood that, individually or in the aggregate, they would influence the judgment made by a reasonable user based on the financial statements." Note that the current definition of materiality does not include the phrase "substantial likelihood" and states that misstatements are considered to be material if they can reasonably be expected to influence the economic decisions of users of the financial statements. The new definition also states that materiality judgments involve both quantitative and qualitative considerations.

STUDY QUESTIONS

1. Which SAS made recent amendments to the concept of materiality?

   a. SAS No. 132

   b. SAS No. 134

   c. SAS No. 137

   d. SAS No. 138

2. SAS No. 138 is effective for periods ending, or for practitioners' examination or review reports dated, on or after:

   a. December 15, 2020

   b. December 15, 2021

   c. December 15, 2022

   d. December 15, 2023

3. Which of the following organizations refers to the concept of something being material if "there is a substantial likelihood that a reasonable person would consider it important"?

   a. Corporate Reporting Dialogue

   b. U.S. Supreme Court

   c. U.S. Securities and Exchange Commission

   d. IFRS Foundation

¶ 405 CHANGES FOR AUDITORS

The following are the AU-C sections that have been amended by SAS No. 138:

- AU-C Section 200, *Overall Objectives of the Independent Auditor and the Conduct of an Audit in Accordance With Generally Accepted Auditing Standards*
- AU-C Section 320, *Materiality in Planning and Performing an Audit*
- AU-C Section 450, *Evaluation of Misstatements Identified During the Audit*
- AU-C Section 600, *Special Considerations—Audits of Group Financial Statements (Including the Work of Component Auditors)*
- AU-C Section 700, *Forming an Opinion and Reporting on Financial Statements* (as amended by SAS No. 134)
- AU-C Section 703, *Forming an Opinion and Reporting on Financial Statements of Employee Benefit Plans Subject to ERISA* (based on SAS No. 136 of the same title)

SAS No. 138 revises the existing language in these AU-C sections regarding misstatements to generally state that "misstatements, including omissions, are considered to be material *if there is a substantial likelihood that*, individually or in the aggregate, *they would influence the judgment made by a reasonable user based on the financial statements*" [emphasis added]. The previous guidance does not include the phrase "substantial likelihood" and indicates that misstatements are considered to be material if they could reasonably be expected to influence the economic decisions of users of the financial statements. These changes are effective for audits of financial statements for periods ending on or after December 15, 2021.

¶ 406 CHANGES TO ATTESTATION

This section of the chapter addresses changes to attestation under the AT-C Sections that have been amended by SSAE No. 20, along with the principal extant guidance addressing materiality and the corresponding amendment of such guidance under SSAE No. 20.

AT-C 205, *Examination Engagements*

Under existing guidance, "Misstatements, including omissions, are considered to be material if, individually or in the aggregate, they could reasonably be expected to influence the relevant decisions of intended users that are made based on the subject matter." SSAE No. 20 amends that guidance as follows: "Misstatements, including omissions, are considered to be material if *there is a substantial likelihood* [emphasis added] that, individually or in the aggregate, they would influence the judgment made by intended users based on the subject matter." This amendment is effective for practitioners' examination reports dated on or after December 15, 2021.

AT-C Section 210, *Review Engagements*

Similarly, SSAE No. 20 amended this section to include the "substantial likelihood" language. The amended standard reads as follows: "Misstatements, including omissions, are considered to be material if there is a substantial likelihood that, individually or in the aggregate, they would influence the judgment made by intended users based on the subject matter." This change also applies to practitioners' review report dated on or after December 15, 2021.

¶ 407 SSARS NO. 25

In February 2020, the AICPA Accounting and Review Services Committee (ARSC) issued Statement on Standards for Accounting and Review Services (SSARS) No. 25, *Materiality in a Review of Financial Statements and Adverse Conclusions*, to converge AR-C section 90, *Review of Financial Statements*, with International Standard for Review Engagements (ISRE) 2400 (Revised), *Engagements to Review Historical Financial Statements*. According to the ARSC, it believes the SSARS requirements should be closely converged with ISRE 2400 (Revised) to help accountants perform and report on engagements in accordance with both sets of standards. The hope is that this convergence will alleviate any confusion regarding the level of assurance obtained in accordance with either set of standards.

SSARS No. 25 requires that an accountant must determine materiality for the financial statements as a whole and apply this materiality when designing procedures and evaluating their results. When obtaining sufficient appropriate review evidence as a basis for a conclusion on the financial statements as a whole, the accountant also must design and perform the analytical procedures and inquires to address all material items in the financial statements, including disclosures.

Further, SSARS No. 25 also aligns more closely with other principles of generally accepted auditing standards (GAAS). Although there are significant differences between an audit engagement and an engagement performed in accordance with SSARS, other concepts, such as materiality, are consistent regardless of the level of services performed on the financial statements.

SSARS No. 25 amends SSARS No. 21, *Statements on Standards for Accounting and Review Services: Clarification and Recodification*, specifically:

- AR-C Section 60, *General Principles for Engagements Performed in Accordance With Statements on Standards for Accounting and Review Services*
- AR-C Section 70, *Preparation of Financial Statements*
- AR-C Section 80, *Compilation Engagements*
- AR-C Section 90, *Review of Financial Statements*

The SSARS No. 25 amendments are effective for engagements performed in accordance with SSARSs on financial statements for periods ending on or after December 15, 2021. Early implementation is permitted.

The definitions of the following terms in AR-C section 60 have been revised to be consistent with the definitions in Statements on Auditing Standards:

- **Applicable financial reporting framework.** The financial reporting framework adopted by management and, when appropriate, those charged with governance in the preparation and fair presentation of the financial statements that is acceptable in view of the nature of the entity and the objective of the financial statements, or that is required by law or regulation.

- **Designated accounting standard-setter.** A body designated by the Council of the AICPA to promulgate accounting principles generally accepted in the United States of America pursuant to the "Compliance With Standards Rule."

- **Financial statements.** A structured representation of historical financial information, including disclosures, intended to communicate an entity's economic resources and obligations at a point in time, or the changes therein for a period of time, in accordance with a financial reporting framework. The term *financial statements* ordinarily refers to a complete set of financial statements as determined by the requirements of the applicable financial reporting framework but can also refer to a single financial statement. Disclosures comprise explanatory or descriptive information, set out as required, expressly permitted, or otherwise allowed by the applicable financial reporting framework, on the face of a financial statement or in the notes, or incorporated therein by reference.

- **General purpose financial statements.** Financial statements prepared in accordance with a general purpose framework.

- **General purpose framework.** A financial reporting framework designed to meet the common financial information needs of a wide range of users.

- **Special purpose financial statements.** Financial statements prepared in accordance with a special purpose framework.

- **Special purpose framework.** A financial reporting framework other than GAAP that is one of the following bases of accounting:

  — *Cash basis.* A basis of accounting that the entity uses to record cash receipts and disbursements and modifications of the cash basis having substantial support (e.g., recording depreciation on fixed assets).

  — *Tax basis.* A basis of accounting that the entity uses to file its tax return for the period covered by the financial statements.

  — *Regulatory basis.* A basis of accounting that the entity uses to comply with the requirements or financial reporting provisions of a regulatory agency to whose jurisdiction the entity is subject (e.g., a basis of accounting that insurance companies use pursuant to the accounting practices prescribed or permitted by a state insurance department).

— *Contractual basis.* A basis of accounting that the entity uses to comply with an agreement between the entity and one or more third parties other than the accountant.

— *Other basis.* A basis of accounting that uses a definite set of logical, reasonable criteria that is applied to all material items appearing in financial statements, for example, the AICPA's Financial Reporting Framework for Small- and Medium-Sized Entities.

AR-C Section 90 has been revised to state that:

- "In a review of financial statements, the accountant expresses a conclusion regarding the entity's financial statements in accordance with an applicable financial reporting framework.

- The accountant's conclusion is based on the accountant obtaining limited assurance."

The following definition of *limited assurance* has been added to AR-C Section 90: "A level of assurance that is less than the reasonable assurance obtained in an audit engagement but is at an acceptable level as the basis for the conclusion expressed in the accountant's review report."

AR-C Section 90 also states that if the accountant determines, or is otherwise aware, that the financial statements are materially misstated, he or she should express one of the following:

- A *qualified conclusion*, concluding that the effects of the matter or matters giving rise to the modification are material but not pervasive to the financial statements

- An *adverse conclusion*, concluding that the effects of the matter or matters giving rise to the modification are both material and pervasive to the financial statements.

¶ 408 ACCOUNTANT'S REVIEW REPORT ILLUSTRATION

In SSARS No. 25, the ARSC provided the following example of a report on comparative financial statements prepared in accordance with U.S. generally accepted accounting principles (GAAP) when a review has been performed for both periods. Notice that the heading "Independent Accountant's Review Report" appears first, followed by the appropriate address. Because this is a report, not a letter, no inside address is included.

If there is a negotiation in process related to the audited company being acquired that makes its outlook either more or less viable as a going concern, does management need to disclose that? If they are discussing going concerns and the accountant deems it is something that might create a going concern, yes, management would need to disclose that. Sometimes people will hold up issuing the review report until this issue is resolved and then make a determination at that point in time. That is acceptable as long as it is done within a reasonable period of time, but it may require a bit of judgment on the accountant's part and perhaps management's part.

Independent Accountant's Review Report

[Appropriate Addressee]

I (We) have reviewed the accompanying financial statements of XYZ Company, which comprise the balance sheets as of December 31, 20X2 and 20X1, and the related statements of income, changes in stockholders' equity, and cash flows for the years then ended, and the related notes to the financial statements. A review includes primarily applying analytical procedures to management's (owners') financial data and making inquiries of company management (owners). A review is substantially less in scope than an audit, the objective of which is the expression of an opinion regarding the financial statements as a whole. Accordingly, I (we) do not express such an opinion.

Management's Responsibility for the Financial Statements

Management (Owners) is (are) responsible for the preparation and fair presentation of these financial statements in accordance with accounting principles generally accepted in the United States of America; this includes the design, implementation, and maintenance of internal control relevant to the preparation and fair presentation of financial statements that are free from material misstatement whether due to fraud or error.

Accountant's Responsibility

My (Our) responsibility is to conduct the review engagements in accordance with Statements on Standards for Accounting and Review Services promulgated by the Accounting and Review Services Committee of the AICPA. Those standards require me (us) to perform procedures to obtain limited assurance as a basis for reporting whether I am (we are) aware of any material modifications that should be made to the financial statements for them to be in accordance with accounting principles generally accepted in the United States of America. I (We) believe that the results of my (our) procedures provide a reasonable basis for my (our) conclusion.

We are required to be independent of XYZ Company and to meet our other ethical responsibilities, in accordance with the relevant ethical requirements related to our reviews.

Accountant's Conclusion

Based on my (our) reviews, I am (we are) not aware of any material modifications that should be made to the accompanying financial statements in order for them to be in accordance with accounting principles generally accepted in the United States of America.

[*Signature of accounting firm or accountant, as appropriate*]

[*Accountant's city and state*]

[*Date of the accountant's review report*]

STUDY QUESTIONS

4. Which of the following was released by the AICPA related to materiality in a review of financial statements and adverse conclusions?

    a. SSARS No. 21

    b. SSARS No. 23

    c. SSARS No. 24

    d. SSARS No. 25

5. As defined within SSARS No. 25, which of the following identifies a basis of accounting that the entity uses to comply with the requirements or financial reporting provisions of a regulatory agency?

    a. Cash basis

    b. Regulatory basis

    c. Tax basis

    d. Contractual basis

6. Which AR-C Section amended by SSARS No. 25 relates to a review of financial statements?

    a. Section 60

    b. Section 70

    c. Section 80

    d. Section 90

MODULE 2: TOP AUDITING ISSUES— CHAPTER 5: Management Discussion and Analysis (MD&A)

¶ 501 WELCOME

On January 30, 2020, the Securities and Exchange Commission (SEC) proposed amendments to eliminate certain duplicative disclosures and enhance disclosures in the Management's Discussion and Analysis of Financial Condition and Results of Operations (MD&A) section for the financial statements. The SEC also proposed parallel amendments applicable to financial disclosures provided by foreign private issuers. This chapter will provide an overview of important concepts and updates related to MD&A as outlined in Topic 9 of the Financial Reporting Manual.

¶ 502 LEARNING OBJECTIVES

Upon completion of this chapter, you will be able to:

- Identify the purpose and objectives of Management Discussion and Analysis (MD&A)
- Understand the typical components included in MD&A
- Identify the updated objective of MD&A disclosures
- Examine details of final amendments
- Examine criteria related to key performance indicators

¶ 503 INTRODUCTION

Management Discussion and Analysis, typically referred to as MD&A, is the portion of a public company's annual report (or quarterly filing) in which management addresses the company's performance. It is intended to be a narrative explanation of the financial statements and statistical data the registrant believes will enhance a readers' understanding of its financial condition along with results of operations. A registrant is defined as:

- An issuer making an initial filing, including amendments, under the Securities Act of 1933 or the Securities Exchange Act of 1934 ("Exchange Act"); or
- A registrant that files periodic reports under the Investment Company Act.

The SEC is responsible for overseeing public companies' compliance with U.S. securities laws and ensuring investors are given adequate information about companies they are investing in.

MD&A can also include a discussion of compliance, risks, and future plans, such as goals and new projects. The requirements for MD&A are outlined in the SEC's Regulation S-K and Regulation S-X.

- **Regulation S-K** is a prescribed regulation under the U.S. Securities Act of 1933 that lays out reporting requirements for various SEC filings used by public companies. Regulation S-K is generally focused on qualitative descriptions. It was adopted in 1977 to foster uniform and integrated disclosure for registration statements under both the Securities Act and the Exchange Act. In 1982, the

SEC expanded and reorganized Regulation S-K to be the central repository for its non-financial statement disclosure requirements.

- **Regulation S-X** is a prescribed regulation in the United States that lays out the specific form and content of financial reports, specifically the financial statements of public companies.

Objectives of MD&A

The SEC's purpose for MD&A disclosures was originally outlined in the following objectives:

- To provide a narrative explanation of a company's financial statements that enables investors to see the company through the eyes of management;
- To enhance overall financial disclosure and provide the context within which financial information should be analyzed; and
- To provide information about the quality of, and potential variability of, a company's earnings and cash flow so that investors can ascertain the likelihood that past performance is indicative of future performance.

The SEC has been continually reviewing the disclosure requirements to improve issuer disclosures of material information while allowing investors to make better capital allocation decisions all while reducing compliance burdens and costs.

STUDY QUESTION

1. What is the purpose of Regulation S-K?
   a. It lays out reporting requirements for various SEC filings used by public companies.
   b. It lays out the specific form and content of financial reports, specifically the financial statements of public companies.
   c. It lays out reporting requirements for the Form 10-K filing used by public companies.
   d. It lays out the specific form and content of financial reports for non-public companies.

¶ 504 OVERVIEW

MD&A is one of many sections required by the SEC and the Financial Accounting Standards Board (FASB) to be included in a public company's annual report to shareholders.

Private entities are not required to draft an MD&A; however, some choose to include it as clarification information for their readers. The SEC has repeatedly stated that MD&A is the "heart and soul" of a company's disclosure requirements under the Securities Exchange Act of 1934. It is a crucial component in increasing the transparency of a company's financial performance and providing investors with the ability to evaluate the company on an informed basis.

During the 2008 recession, the SEC brought numerous enforcement actions against public companies and their chief executive and financial officers for allegedly failing to properly fulfill their MD&A disclosure requirements. Companies should carefully review their procedures for preparing MD&A. Simply relying on what was done last year may not be enough.

The overview of MD&A includes information about how economic or government changes have affected or might affect the company. In the end, the overall focus is on items that might have a material effect on the company while providing a fundamental analysis of the company's results of operations. MD&A represents the thoughts and opinions of management and provides a forecast of future operations. The discussion provided by management is intended to identify information that interested parties might not easily identify from a review of the quantitative information in the financial statements. Since MD&A is management's opinion, these statements cannot typically be authenticated and therefore the MD&A section is not audited. The MD&A section is required to meet certain standards. The FASB indicates that "MD&A should provide a balanced presentation that includes both positive and negative information about the topics discussed."

Statements must be based in fact, and there must be an attempt to paint a balanced picture of the company's future prospects.

Disclosure Components

The following components are typically included in most MD&A disclosures:

Executive overview and outlook. In this section of a company's MD&A, management discusses the company's financial objectives, its plans for growth, and its successes in the past period along with its risks and challenges. It is intended to provide a "big-picture" outlook of the company's operations. Although this section is not a required component of MD&A, it is commonly included because it provides a good background and sets the stage for the remaining information the company will present. Often, a synopsis of the company's recent history and business activity is used as a precursor for presenting the financial results. In addition, this section may include summary information on recent mergers or acquisitions and how they impact performance. This is important for gaining an understanding of the company's current operating and financial position.

Operating results. In this section, management summarizes critical information from the financial reports and provides a verbal interpretation of the financial statement numbers. This section may include an explanation of significant changes from prior periods as well as uncertainties that may be foreseen that could impact future business operations. Management may also include forecasted information, economic drivers, or other information it feels may be useful to the reader. This section may include both narrative and table formatted data.

Trends and risks. Management is required to discuss trends and risks that might affect future performance. An analysis of the potential positive or negative consequences of certain events is considered important to assist current and potential investors in their understanding of the company's position.

An important example in relation to trends and risks is the COVID-19 pandemic. The SEC has acknowledged the impact of COVID-19 on companies is evolving rapidly and its future effects are uncertain. The SEC is monitoring how companies are reporting the effects and risks on their businesses, financial condition, and results of operations and providing guidance as companies prepare disclosure documents during this uncertain time. The SEC encourages timely reporting but recognizes it may be difficult to assess or predict the broad effects of COVID-19 on industries or individual companies. Nevertheless, the effects COVID-19 has had on a company, what management expects its future impact will be, how management is responding to evolving events, and how it is planning for COVID-19-related uncertainties can be material to investment and voting decisions, so companies are strongly encouraged to consider their disclosures.

Litigation. MD&A must disclose any current or possible litigation and how it might have an impact on the company's financial stability. If there is litigation in process, analysis should assess whether management believes there is any merit in the legal actions and the expected outcome of those actions. Often, management will utilize scenarios and probabilities when presenting the potential outcomes of litigation so that investors have a full overview of risk as the organization sees it.

Liquidity and capital resources. In 2003 and again in 2010, the SEC provided updated guidance intended to improve the discussion of liquidity and capital resources. Generally, this section is dedicated to explaining and analyzing the company's cash needs from both a short-term and a long-term perspective.

Information included will discuss the company's level of liquidity, its ability to access capital, its level of profitability, and the likelihood that the rate of growth or earnings will continue. Any material capital repayments due in the near future will be considered within this discussion. Management will also highlight certain debt covenants or repayment structures that will affect the company's ability to meet its cash goals. Other important trends and uncertainties relating to liquidity might include difficulties accessing the debt markets, reliance on commercial paper or other short-term financing arrangements, maturity mismatches between borrowing sources and the assets funded by those sources, changes in terms requested by counterparties, changes in the valuation of collateral, and counterparty risk.

> **NOTE:** The absence of specific references in existing disclosure requirements for off-balance sheet arrangements or contractual obligations to repurchase transactions that are accounted for as sales, or to any other transfers of financial assets that are accounted for as sales, does not relieve the registrant from disclosure under liquidity and capital resources.

Off-balance sheet arrangements. This addition to MD&A was approved in 2003. At that time, the amendments approved by the SEC required a registrant to provide an explanation of its off-balance sheet arrangements in a separately captioned subsection of the MD&A section in its disclosure documents.

Off-balance sheet arrangements are transactions or agreements that are not required to be reported on the balance sheet. These arrangements can impact revenues, expenses, and cash flows. Off-balance sheet items are in contrast to loans, debt, and equity, which do appear on the balance sheet. Common examples of off-balance sheet items include research and development partnerships, joint ventures, and operating leases.

Any off-balance sheet arrangements that have been issued to secure business dealings must be disclosed by management. In addition, management should discuss any derivative instruments (e.g., hedge contracts) the company has entered into as an attempt to reduce the potential risk of price fluctuations or exchange rate variations. Typically, these contractual obligations influence how the company conducts business and are critical to provide investors with relevant information for understanding the organization's overall business. Management's discussion will include information about these arrangements and how they may serve the business as well as how they will affect credit risk.

Generally, off-balance sheet arrangements include the following categories of contractual arrangements:

- Certain guarantee contracts
- Retained or contingent interests in assets transferred to an unconsolidated entity

- Derivative instruments that are classified as equity
- Material variable interests in unconsolidated entities that conduct certain activities.

Critical accounting estimates (CAEs). This analysis evaluates any material accounting estimates that may be included in the financial statements. An accounting estimate is when management makes an approximation of an element in the financial statements. An example may be an estimate by a manufacturer of future product returns. In determining whether the estimate is "critical," management should consider:

- Did the accounting estimate require the company to make assumptions about matters that were *highly uncertain* at the time the accounting estimate was made?
- Would different estimates that the company *reasonably could have used* in the current period, or changes *in* the accounting estimate that are *reasonably likely to occur* from period to period, have a material impact on the presentation of financial condition or results of operations?

The number of CAEs varies by company. The SEC expects that most companies have between three to five CAEs. The information provides an analysis on how these estimates could affect operating results. Also, because many estimates can be used in developing the financial statements, management should disclose the degree of certainty associated with the estimates and the impact on the company if the estimates turn out to be in error.

Disclosure about CAEs involve the following three fundamental elements:

- Basic disclosure necessary to understand the CAEs
- Sensitivity of reported operating results and financial condition to changes in CAEs or their underlying assumptions
- Senior management's discussion of the development, selection, and disclosure of CAEs with the audit committee

STUDY QUESTIONS

2. What is the purpose for including an executive overview and outlook within MD&A disclosures?

   a. To provide detailed information about the operations of the organization

   b. To provide a "big-picture" outlook of the company's operations

   c. To provide detailed information about how the organization finances its operations

   d. To provide detailed information about critical estimates made by management

3. What are off-balance sheet arrangements?

   a. Transactions that appear on the income statement

   b. Transactions that only appear in the cash flow statement

   c. Transactions that are not part of the parent company

   d. Transactions or agreements that are not required to be reported on the balance sheet

Updated MD&A Objectives

In 2003, the SEC issued an interpretive release with the intent to elicit more meaningful disclosure in a number of MD&A areas. These areas included the overall presentation and focus of MD&A. There was a general emphasis on the discussion and analysis of known trends, demands, commitments, events, and uncertainties, and specific guidance on disclosures about liquidity, capital resources, and CAEs.

On January 30, 2020, the SEC proposed amendments to eliminate certain duplicative disclosures and promote disclosures in the MD&A section. These amendments are more tailored to a registrant's businesses, facts, and circumstances. Also on January 30, the SEC provided new guidance on the disclosure of key performance indicators and metrics in MD&A. A week earlier, the SEC's Division of Corporation Finance issued three new Compliance & Disclosure Interpretations (C&DIs) addressing the omission, under recent rule changes, of the MD&A discussion for the earliest of three years.

The 2020 proposed amendments would codify elements of the 2003 guidance. Item 303(a) (outlining requirements for MD&A) would set out the "objective" of MD&A to provide both a historical and prospective analysis of the registrant's financial condition and results of operations. There would be particular emphasis on the registrant's prospects for the future. Key objectives of MD&A to be emphasized under the new amended rule include:

- Material information relevant to an assessment of the financial condition and results of operations of the registrant. This includes an evaluation of the amounts and certainty of cash flows from operations and from outside sources.
- Material financial and statistical data the registrant believes will enhance a reader's understanding of the financial condition, changes in financial condition, and results of operations.
- Material events and uncertainties known to management that would cause reported financial information not to be necessarily indicative of future operating results or of future financial condition. This would include descriptions and amounts of matters that:
  - Would have a material impact on future operations that may not have had an impact in the past, and
  - Have had a material impact on reported operations and are not expected to have an impact on future operations.

The amendments will significantly revise existing MD&A requirements and improve disclosures for investors and reduce the compliance burden for companies.

Amendments

Following is an explanation of the item areas specifically outlined for elimination or change under the final adopted amendments. Also included is a description of the required previous disclosure, the adopted change, and the reason for change.

2020 SEC Amendments

Item 301, Selected Financial Data	
Original Disclosure Purpose	This disclosure required businesses to furnish (in comparative columnar form) selected financial data that highlighted trends in financial condition including: • Each of the last five fiscal years of the registrant • Any additional fiscal years necessary to keep information from being misleading Some exceptions were provided for smaller registrants and emerging growth companies.
Adopted Change	The SEC has eliminated the reference to year-to-year comparisons. Instruction 1 of Item 301 will now state that registrants may use any presentation that, in their judgment, enhances a reader's understanding of the company's financial condition, changes in financial condition, and results of operations. In addition, the SEC deleted the reference to five-year selected financial data in Instruction 1 to Item 303(a). Item 303(a)(3)(ii) already requires disclosure of known trends and uncertainties. Revisions to this item allow registrants providing financial statements covering three years in a filing to omit discussion of the earliest of the three years. This is allowable only if the discussion was already included in another of the registrant's prior filings on EDGAR that required disclosure in compliance with Item 303 of Regulation S-K. Registrants electing not to include a discussion of the earliest year and who rely on this instruction must identify the location in the prior filing where the omitted discussion can be found. The SEC also expanded the condition regarding the earliest year discussion to allow registrants to rely on any prior EDGAR filings that include these discussions. There was not an adoption, as an explicit condition, that the omitted discussion must not be "material to an understanding" of the registrant's financial condition, changes in financial condition, and results of operations. This change recognizes the original language was superfluous and never intended to modify, supplement, or alter the overarching materiality analysis.
Reason for Change	The reason for the elimination of "Selected Financial Data and Supplementary Financial Information" is because the information is already available in a company's filings. The information required in this disclosure was considered duplicative. When the precursor to Item 301 was adopted in 1970, prior annual reports were not quickly and easily accessible. This has changed with the advancement in technology. The change will also modernize and simplify disclosure requirements.
Item 301(b), Application to Foreign Private Issuers	
Adopted Change	The amendment provides that when a filing includes financial statements covering three years, discussion about the earliest year may be omitted if the discussion was already included in the registrant's prior year Form 20-F filed on EDGAR or in any other of the registrant's prior filings on EDGAR that required disclosure. Registrants electing not to include a discussion of the earliest year must, however, include a statement that identifies the location in the prior filing where the omitted discussion may be found.

2020 SEC Amendments	
Item 302(a), Supplementary Financial Information	
Original Disclosure Purpose	This disclosure included: • Disclosure of net sales, gross profit, and income/loss from continuing operations • Per share data, net income (loss) attributable to the registrant for each full quarter within the two most recent fiscal years • Per share data for any subsequent interim period where financial statements are included or required to be included
Adopted Change	Registrants are no longer required to provide two years of selected quarterly financial data. This is in alignment with the SEC's FAST (Fixing America's Surface Transportation) Act–related amendments to Regulation S-K, Item 303(a). Those changes now permit a company (in a filing providing three years of financial statements) to omit the MD&A discussion of the earliest year if the discussion appears in a prior filing on EDGAR and the company includes a statement identifying where the omitted discussion may be found. The FAST Act was adopted in April 2019 to modernize and simplify disclosure requirements for public companies, investment advisors, and investment companies. The amendments generally streamline or abridge disclosure requirements and, notably, shorten MD&A and eliminate confidential treatment requests for material contracts in many circumstances. On January 24, 2020, the SEC's Division of Corporation Finance issued three new Regulation S-K Compliance Disclosures and Interpretations (C&DIs) to assist companies as they evaluate whether to take advantage of this new disclosure flexibility in upcoming annual reports on Form 10-K. C&DI's were last updated in 2017. They comprise the Division's interpretations of the rules adopted under the Securities Act. The guidance offers two principal takeaways: • The identifying cross-reference does not incorporate the earlier discussion by reference unless the company expressly provides so. This is true for references to annual reports and registration statements that incorporate the annual reports by reference. • A company may not omit an earlier period discussion (or presumably any portion of the discussion) that is necessary to an understanding of its financial condition, changes in financial condition, and results of operations. Whether there is a difference between a discussion that is "necessary to an understanding" and one that is "necessary to make what was said not misleading" is questionable. Any question about whether the earliest year has information that is meaningfully different from the two most recent years should be resolved by including it or incorporating it by reference.
Reason for Change	Reduce repetition and focus disclosure on material information. Modernize disclosure requirement in light of technological developments.
Item 302(b), Supplementary Financial Information	
Original Disclosure Purpose	This disclosure was for registrants engaged in oil and gas-producing activities required to disclose information about those activities for each period presented.
Adopted Change	Eliminate this requirement.

2020 SEC Amendments	
Reason for Change	Minimize duplication.
Item 303(a), MD&A	
Original Disclosure Purpose	This item covered disclosures on discussion of off balance-sheet arrangements, disclosures related to a table of contractual obligations, and disclosures related to the impact of inflation and changing prices.
Adopted change	The change was to clarify the objective of MD&A toward a more principles-based approach. In relation to Item 303, the proposals would provide for the changes bulleted below. The following bulleted changes are further described in the succeeding sections. • Add a new Item 303(a) to state the principal objectives of MD&A including full fiscal years and interim periods. This will incorporate much of the Instructions in 1, 2, and 3 to better emphasize the objective of MD&A for both full fiscal years and interim periods. Items 303(a) and (b) will be recaptioned as Items 303(b) and (c). • Eliminate unnecessary cross-references and remove outdated and duplicative language. • Update capital resource disclosures. Registrants will now be required to disclosure material cash requirements (including commitments for capital expenditures as of the latest fiscal period), the anticipated source of funds needed to satisfy cash requirements, and the general purpose of such requirements. • Update the results of operations disclosure to require disclosure of known events that are reasonably likely to cause a material change in relationship between costs/revenues. • Revise the interim MD&A requirement in Item 303(b) to provide flexibility by allowing companies to compare their most recently completed quarter to either the corresponding quarter of the prior year (as is currently required) or to the immediately preceding quarter. • Eliminate the requirement to discuss the impact of inflation. • Replace the specific requirement to disclose off-balance sheet arrangements with a directive to disclose arrangements in the broader context of the MD&A discussion. • Add a requirement to discuss CAEs, to clarify and codify SEC guidance on CAEs. • Add the flexibility to choose whether to compare the same quarter from the prior year, or the immediately preceding quarter. • Replace Item 303(a)(4), Off-Balance Sheet Arrangements, with a principles-based instruction about the need to discuss off-balance sheet arrangements in the broader context of MD&A. • Eliminate current Item 303(c), Safe Harbor, in light of the replacement of Item 303(a)(4) and elimination of Item 303(a)(5). • Eliminate Item 303(d), Smaller Reporting Companies, in light of the elimination of Items 303(a)(3)(iv) and 303(a)(5).
Reason for Change	Simplify and enhance the purpose of MD&A.
Item 303(a)(2), Capital Resources	
Original Disclosure Purpose	This disclosure was used to describe any known material trends in the registrant's capital resources. The registrant would indicate any expected material changes and the relative cost of the resources. The discussion considered changes between equity, debt, and any off-balance sheet financing arrangements.
Adopted Change	Updated capital resource disclosures to require disclosure of material cash requirements including commitments for capital expenditures as of the latest fiscal period, the anticipated source of funds needed to satisfy cash requirements, and the general purpose of such requirements.

2020 SEC Amendments	
Reason for Change	To revise the disclosure requirements to account for capital expenditures that are not necessarily capital investments. This assists in recognizing that expenditures for human capital or intellectual property have become increasingly important for some companies. Amendment will also add product lines, as an example, of other subdivisions that may need to be discussed where necessary to understand a company's business.
Item 303(a)(3)(ii), Results of Operations	
Original Disclosure Purpose	To the extent financial statements disclose material increases in net sales or revenues, registrant provided a narrative discussion of the extent to which increases were attributable to increases in prices, volume or amount of goods or services being sold, or the introduction of new products or services.
Adopted Change	Update the results of operations disclosure to require disclosure of known events that are *reasonably likely* to cause a material change in the relationship between costs and revenues. An example would be known or reasonably likely future increases in costs of labor or materials or price increases. Clarify that a discussion of the reasons underlying material changes in net sales or revenues is required.
Reason for Change	Clarify requirement by using threshold of "*reasonably likely*," consistent with the SEC's interpretative guidance on forward-looking statements. The change related to clarification of discussion of the reasons for underlying material change will codify existing SEC MD&A guidance.
Item 303(a)(3)(iv), Results of Operations (Inflation and Price Changes)	
Original Disclosure Purpose	For the three most recent fiscal years, or for those fiscal years in which the registrant has been engaged in business, they would discuss the impact of inflation and changing prices on net sales and revenues and on income from continuing operations.
Adopted Change	This item is eliminated. Registrants are still required to discuss these matters if they are part of a known trend or uncertainty that has had, or registrant reasonably expects to have, a material favorable/ unfavorable impact on net sales, or revenue, or income from continuing operations.
Reason for Change	Encourage registrants to focus on material information that is tailored to a registrant's businesses, facts, and circumstances.
Item 303(a)(4), Off-Balance Sheet Arrangement	
Original Disclosure Purpose	This item focused on off-balance sheet arrangements that have (or are reasonably likely to have) a current/future effect on registrant's financial condition, changes in financial condition, revenues or expenses, results of operations, liquidity, capital expenditures, or capital resources material to investors.

2020 SEC Amendments	
Adopted Change	The specific requirement to disclose off-balance sheet arrangements was replaced with a directive to disclose the arrangements in the broader context of the MD&A discussion. Areas the registrants were directed to discuss included commitments/obligations arising from arrangements with unconsolidated entities or persons that have, or are reasonably likely to have, a material current or future effect on the following areas for the registrant: • Financial condition • Changes in financial condition • Revenues or expenses • Results of operations • Liquidity • Cash requirements • Capital resources even when the arrangement results in no obligation being reported in the registrant's consolidated balance sheets. Registrants would no longer be required to provide a contractual obligations table.
Reason for Change	To prompt registrants to consider and integrate disclosure of off-balance sheet arrangements within the context of their MD&A.

Item 303(a)(5), Contractual Obligations

Original Disclosure Purpose	Under this item, the registrant had to disclose known contractual obligations in tabular format. There was no materiality threshold for the disclosure.
Adopted Change	Registrants are not required to provide a contractual obligations table.
Reason for Change	The elimination of the contractual obligations table is attributed to is overlap with information already required in the financial statements and the goal of promoting a principles-based approach to MD&A. It would also promote the principles-based nature of MD&A and simplify disclosures by reducing redundancy.

Material Changes In Line Items

Adopted Change	This change moved a portion of the current Instruction 4 into a new Item 303(b). This was to clarify that where there are material changes in a line item (including where material changes within a line item offset one another), disclosure of the underlying reasons for these material changes in quantitative and qualitative terms is required.
Reason for Change	Enhance the analysis in MD&A and clarify MD&A disclosure requirements by codifying existing SEC guidance on the importance of analysis in MD&A.

Item 303(b), Interim Periods

Adopted Change	Registrants would be permitted to compare their most recently completed quarter to either the corresponding quarter of the prior year or the immediately preceding quarter.
Reason for Change	This would allow for flexibility in comparison of interim periods to enhance the disclosure provided to investors.

Critical Accounting Estimates

Original Purpose	In 2001, the SEC reminded registrants that, under the existing MD&A disclosure requirements, a registrant should address material implications of uncertainties associated with the methods, assumptions, and estimates underlying the registrant's critical accounting measurements.

2020 SEC Amendments	
Adopted Change	The change explicitly requires disclosure of CAEs. Item 303(b)(4) now places the requirement to discuss CAEs at the heart of MD&A by requiring the following: • A discussion, to the extent material, as to why each CAE is subject to uncertainty, how much each estimate has changed during the reporting period, and the sensitivity of the reported amount to the methods, assumptions, and estimates underlying its calculation. • Quantitative as well as qualitative information, when quantitative information is reasonably available and would provide material information to investors. The instruction to Item 303(b)(4) states that the disclosure of CAEs should "supplement, but not duplicate, the description of accounting policies or other disclosures in the notes to the financial statements." Refinements to existing disclosure requirements: • Requirement of a quantitative and qualitative discussion of material period-to-period changes in financial statement line items, including where material changes within a line item offset one another. • A registrant's discussion of capital resources should include material cash requirements and not just material commitments for capital expenditures. The change is intended to enhance disclosure of a registrant's ability to generate cash and meet its material cash requirements. • Promote meaningful analysis of measurement uncertainties. The standard for disclosing a future event impacting costs or revenues is whether it is "reasonably likely" to have an impact and not the current higher standard of whether it "will" have an impact.
Reason for Change	Facilitate compliance and improve resulting disclosure and eliminate disclosure that duplicates the financial statement discussion of significant policies. This conforms the disclosure standard for future events to the standard for trends and uncertainties and is consistent with providing investors with a better understanding of future prospects.

STUDY QUESTIONS

4. In the update to Item 303, which of the following elements was eliminated?

    a. The requirement to discuss off-balance sheet arrangements

    b. The requirement to discuss the impact of inflation

    c. The requirement to disclose capital resource issues

    d. The requirement to discuss critical accounting estimates

5. Item 303(a)(3)(ii), Results of Operations Disclosure, was changed to focus on which of the following?

    a. Changes that are reasonably likely to cause a material change in the relationship between costs and revenues

    b. Changes that have a significant change to assets and liabilities

    c. Changes that have a significant change to equity

    d. Changes that have a quantifiable significant change in the relationship between costs and revenues

Changes to Key Performance Indicators

On January 30, 2020, the SEC provided new guidance on the disclosure of key performance indicators (KPIs) and metrics in MD&A. Examples of metrics to which the guidance will apply include:

- Operating margin
- Same store sales
- Sales per square foot
- Total customers/subscribers
- Average revenue per user
- Daily/monthly active users/usage
- Active customers
- Net customer additions
- Total impressions
- Number of memberships
- Traffic growth
- Comparable customer transactions increase
- Voluntary or involuntary employee turnover rate
- Percentage breakdown of workforce (e.g., active workforce covered under collective bargaining agreements)
- Total energy consumed

Per the guidance, companies should consider existing MD&A requirements and the specific need for inclusion of any relevant additional information (or KPIs) to ensure the presentation is not misleading. The SEC outlined some items it generally expects to be included for disclosures to accompany any metric:

- A clear definition of the metric and how it is calculated
- A statement indicating the reasons why the metric provides useful information to investors
- A statement indicating how management uses the metric in managing or monitoring the performance of the business.

The guidance also advises that, if a company changes the method used to calculate or presents the metric, it should consider disclosure of the following:

- The differences in the way the metric is calculated or presented compared to prior periods
- The reasons for the change
- The effects of any change on the amounts or other information being disclosed and on amounts or other information previously reported
- Other differences in methodology and results that would reasonably be expected to be relevant to an understanding of the company's performance or prospects.

Depending on the significance of any changes in methodology and results, the company also should consider whether to recast prior metrics to conform to the current presentation and place the current disclosure in an appropriate context. The guidance also indicates that when KPIs and metrics are material to an investment or voting decision, the company should consider whether it has effective disclosure controls and procedures in place to process information related to such items to ensure consistency as well as accuracy.

STUDY QUESTION

6. The SEC outlined items it generally expects to be included for disclosures that should accompany any metric. Which of the following is one of those items?

    a. A clear definition of where the metric came from

    b. A statement indicating the reasons why the metric provides useful information to investors

    c. A statement explaining what reliance the external auditors place on the metric

    d. A statement explaining what reliance investors should place on the metric

Other Key MD&A Modifications

The SEC noted the requirement for the audit reports of large accelerated filers for fiscal years ending on or after June 30, 2019, to include a discussion of critical audit matters (CAMs). The SEC views CAMs as different from CAEs because a CAM is a critical matter involving challenging, subjective, or complex *auditor* judgment, while a CAE involves significant *management* estimates having a material impact on a company's financial condition or operating performance. Accordingly, the SEC does not believe that Item 303(a)(4) would necessarily result in duplicative disclosure.

Effective Date

For the most part, the final rules are effective May 2, 2019.

¶ 505 SUMMARY

Transparent financial reporting that conveys a complete and understandable picture of a company's financial position reduces uncertainty in our markets. Surprises to investors can be reduced or avoided when a company provides clear and understandable information about known trends, events, demands, commitments, and uncertainties, particularly where they are reasonably likely to have a current or future material impact on that company. The economic environment is not static. Circumstances and risks change and, as a result, disclosure about those circumstances and risks must also evolve.

MODULE 2: TOP AUDITING ISSUES— CHAPTER 6: Using Data Analytics in an Audit

¶ 601 WELCOME

This chapter explains how auditors can use data analytics in an audit. Topics discussed include common uses of data analytics, data formats, types of data analysis, analytical procedures, and Benford's Law.

¶ 602 LEARNING OBJECTIVES

Upon completion of this chapter, you will be able to:

- Identify various types of data analytics that can be used in an audit
- Recognize how to use Benford's Law in an analysis of data in an audit situation

¶ 603 INTRODUCTION

Data analytics is the science of analyzing raw data in order to make conclusions about that information, and it can greatly enhance an auditor's ability to conduct an audit. The International Standards for the Professional Practice of Internal Auditing include the following guidance for conducting an internal audit: "In exercising due professional care internal auditors must consider the use of technology-based audit and other data analysis techniques." The standards define *technology-based audit techniques* as "any automated audit tool, such as generalized audit software, test data generators, computerized audit programs, specialized audit utilities, and computer-assisted audit techniques (CAATs)."

Eventually, in my opinion, the American Institute of Certified Public Accountants (AICPA) and the Public Company Accounting Oversight Board (PCAOB) will adopt similar standards so that all auditors use analytics as part of the audit.

Auditors can use data analytics for many different purposes. It can be used to look at tying out general ledger balances and account balances, to look for trends, or to analyze customer accounts. Data analytics can also help auditors perform a quantity and price analysis, as well as verify that sales taxes were properly calculated. Auditors can tie data analytics to artificial intelligence (AI) to uncover unusual transactions or anomalies that need further investigation.

> **COMMENT:** Although some professionals fear that AI and data analytics will eventually eliminate the audit function, I believe a human auditor will always be needed. AI and data analytics can perform repetitive tasks so that auditors can focus on higher level functions that require professional judgment and experience.

Uses for data analytics in an audit include the following:

- Planning or risk assessment
  - Analysis of preliminary general ledger account balances
  - Nonstatistical trend analysis
  - Analysis of customer accounts
  - Quantity and price analysis of sales revenue
  - Process mining from sales order to sales invoice

- Substantive analytical procedures
  - Nonstatistical predictive models
  - Regression analysis
- Test of details
  - Cash receipts to sales invoice matching
  - Three-way match of sales invoice, shipping document, and master price list
- Testing the effectiveness of internal controls

Data analytics typically requires specialized software. Firms have a wide range of data analytics software from which to choose, depending on their firm's size, focus, and budget. Here is just a sampling of the many software options:

- Tableau
- Diver Platform
- Inzata
- Infotools Harmoni
- Zoho Analytics
- Chartio
- Klipfolio
- OpenText Analytics Suite
- EasyMorph
- Scoreboard KPI Management
- Analytics2Insights
- MarketSight
- AnswerRocket
- JPM Statistical Software
- Monarch
- IntilliFront BI
- Cluvio
- AnswerDock
- XLSTAT

Today, businesses are increasingly relying on technology. Large amounts of purchases and transactions are conducted on smartphones and mobile devices. The use of electronic data storage is growing rapidly, as accounting data is stored online in spreadsheets, online documents such as PDFs and Microsoft Word documents, and online databases. Electronic communications—via email, voicemail, text messages, and social media platforms—are on the rise as well. We have access to more data now than ever before, and better tools for analyzing that data. These and many other technologies are affecting the auditing profession. Consider the following:

- **Cloud computing.** Cloud computing allows organizations to use software in the cloud or store data on cloud services, and those may be areas that auditors have to be able to audit.
- **Blockchain.** There is a huge influx of Blockchain technology, and Blockchain is not just for cryptocurrencies. Blockchain was originally designed to verify documents and the dates those documents were stored on a computer. Companies can use Blockchain to verify the dates that contracts were signed, transactions were posted, orders were made, or shipments were shipped.

- **Smart businesses.** "Smart" businesses are using AI to do things like vary the temperature in their office buildings and factories, ramp up or slow down production, automatically schedule maintenance, track inventory, and other automated tasks.

- **Robotics.** Some factories are using robotics for efficiency, but robots can be hacked. How much of the cybersecurity on those robots is safe? Auditors must consider that as part of their audits.

- **Virtual reality.** Organizations are increasingly using virtual reality for training and other purposes.

- **Biometrics.** This technology is commonly used for gaining access to systems using facial recognition, thumbprints or fingerprints, or retina scans.

- **Internet of Things (IoT).** This encompasses all the items that can be connected to the internet, such as printers, scanners, cell phones, tablets, and more. All of these devices store data that may need to be audited.

- **Quantum computers.** These computers, which store data on individual atoms rather than on transistors, should be available in the next few years. They will offer technology that will allow them to decrypt in seconds data that would normally take top supercomputers years to decrypt.

- **Social media.** Social media is a big issue in public company audits. An employee's disclosure of nonpublic information via social media can result in potential insider trading risks.

- **Cryptocurrencies.** More and more states are legalizing the use of cryptocurrencies.

- **XBRL.** The Securities and Exchange Commission (SEC) is using XBRL (eXtensible Business Reporting Language) to standardize reporting under the EDGAR system.

- **Business intelligence (BI).** This allows entities to get real-time data rather than accessing it after the fact.

Other technologies auditors might encounter in their work include self-driving trucks, botnets of things, interactive TV, on-demand services, internet sales, streaming data, and more.

Traditional Analytics Versus Big Data Analytics

Traditional analytics has focused on descriptive analytics and diagnostic analytics, looking at things that happened in the past. Big data analytics, on the other hand, focuses on predictive analytics, predicting what could happen in the future using data science to find anomalies and catch errors and fraud as they occur.

While traditional analytics involves limited data sets, cleansed data, and simple models, big data analytics involves large-scale data sets, more types of data, and complex data models. Big data analytics also looks at correlations to get new insight and more accurate answers. Traditional analytics supports causation, determining what happened and why.

¶ 604 WORKING WITH CLIENT DATA

One of the first things auditors must do when planning an audit is to determine where the client's data is located. Most clients will say their data is on their servers, which is true. There is a large amount of data on their servers. However, clients often have data in other places too, such as their application databases (accounting software), operating software, or sales databases (e.g., SalesForce). They might also have data on storage devices like jump drives and external hard drives, and mobile devices such as tablets and cell phones. Many companies use cloud storage for both internal and external data transfers, or they might use software in the cloud. Knowing the location of the client's backup files is also important. Auditors must identify where all of the client's data is and, of course, document that in their workpapers.

Data Formats

A client's data might exist in several different formats. Physical documents include traditional paper documents such as invoices and contracts. Today, however, most data is electronic. There are two types of electronic data: *structured data* and *unstructured data*. Structured data includes:

- Transactional data (e.g., information in the accounting system)
- Audit trails
- Databases
- Spreadsheets

Unstructured data is information that does not fit in a typical database, such as emails, Word documents, PDF contracts, memos, and data posted on social media. Customer demographic information gathered from a client's website through cookies or other means, or through surveys, is another source of unstructured data.

> **EXAMPLE:** When auditors are auditing revenue recognition, they must be able to identify customer contracts. Those customer contracts—and amendments to them—might be in a PDF document, a Word document, or a scanned document. A contract might be in an email, or in a document signing program on the internet. Auditors must be able to find this data to identify whether all the contracts were input in the system and the revenues properly recognized.

In addition to data formats, auditors should look at the client's:

- **Data volume.** This is the amount of data that is going through the client's system. The auditor should assess how much data exists, as well as the potential value of that data. Not all data has the same value. An organization might collect a great deal of information that is totally worthless to its business.
- **Data velocity.** Data velocity is the speed at which the client generates, collects, and processes data. For example, credit card companies, which process millions of transactions every second, have high data velocity.
- **Data variety.** Clients typically have many different types of data available.
- **Data veracity.** This indicates how good, valid, or accurate the client's data is. Remember the adage "garbage in, garbage out." If bad data goes into the system, it can corrupt the data throughout the entire system. Auditors are responsible for identifying any material misstatement in the financial statements due to errors or fraud. Those can be uncovered through data analytics and audit process.

STUDY QUESTIONS

1. Which of the following is true regarding changing technology in business?
    a. There is a decreasing reliance by business on technology.
    b. We have limited access to data.
    c. Social media poses risks for insider trading.
    d. Blockchain is primarily used for Bitcoin.

2. Data volume is:

   a. The speed at which data is generated

   b. The amount of data that is going through the system

   c. An indication of the different types of data that are available

   d. An indication of how good the data is

Types of Data Analysis

Several types of data analysis are available to auditors when working with client data.

- **Exploratory analysis.** This type of analysis allows auditors to use data that has already been gathered for other reasons. Clients gather a lot of data that auditors can use for audit purposes.

- **Predictive analysis.** Auditors use predictive data to look for where they think things should be, for example, by doing a regression analysis on the allowance for doubtful accounts to determine if the allowance is reasonable. For other allowance accounts, auditors might need to do some type of predictive analysis to determine if the client's estimate of returns and allowances, warranties, bad debt, and so on, is reasonable or if the client is playing with those numbers to smooth their earnings.

- **Descriptive analysis.** Descriptive analysis techniques includes statistics, ratio analysis, and other analyses that auditors perform on a regular basis as part of an audit.

- **Inferential analysis.** This type of analysis encompasses the concept of sampling. If we take a sample of a population, we can infer that the characteristics of that sample are going to be the same as the whole population. This is an important part of the auditor's data analysis.

- **Confirmatory analysis.** This type of analysis is used to confirm numbers and accounts, and make sure that the accounts tie out.

- **Text or number searches.** Text or number searches can be conducted to find duplicate invoices, missing invoice numbers, missing receipt numbers, and so on.

- **Causal analysis.** Auditors use this type of data analysis to find causes. For example, if there are a number of errors in the client's accounts receivable account, the auditor can use data analytics to determine the root of those errors.

Data Integrity

One of the things to remember, both on the client side and the auditor side, is the concept of data integrity. Obviously, the client must ensure it has good, accurate data. And both the client and the auditor must comply with federal and state laws on data security and securing consumer information. Physical data integrity must be maintained for the collection of data, the use of data, the dissemination of data, the storage of data, and the destruction or removal of data.

Auditors should examine the data integrity of the client's systems. How accurate is the client's data? Is the data complete? Is the client consistent in its gathering and use of the data? Does the client have a records retention policy that tells it when to get rid of data? If the auditor is relying on an electronic system like accounting software to produce the information the auditor uses or the client uses to create the financial statements, the auditor needs to ensure that the data is complete—that all the data was input into the system.

¶ 605 COMMON TYPES OF ANALYTICAL PROCEDURES

Auditors can use several types of data analytics tools in the audit process. *Trend analysis* involves looking at trends such as sales trends, return trends, trends in write-offs, and trends for travel and office expenses. This type of analysis can uncover major changes or changes that are occurring faster than normal for the companies the auditor benchmarks for the client.

Most auditors are familiar with *ratio analysis*, which is typically addressed in college-level accounting courses. *Nonstatistical predictive modeling* is a method auditors can use to predict where things should be and then compare that to what is actually booked in the client's system to identify if there are any variances. For example, an auditor can use nonstatistical predictive modeling to predict patterns in rent for property management companies or to predict electrical usage or water usage for utility companies. *Descriptive statistics* involves concepts such as the mean, mode, median, and standard deviation, with which auditors should be familiar.

Regression analysis is the most complex type of analytical procedure auditors use and is performed using software. With this method, auditors can identify the accuracy of a client's estimates. Regression analysis can be used to determine various statistical measures, such as R2 (coefficient of determination), T-statistics, and standard error. It can also be used for correlations. For an electric company, for example, one would expect a spike in temperatures to cause a spike in electric usage. In addition, regression analysis is often applied for hypothesis testing, which is used to test internal controls.

Distribution of Data

When auditors and accountants look at data, typically it is normally distributed. In a *normal distribution*, 99.7 percent of data points are within three standard deviations from the mean, 95 percent are within two standard deviations, and 68 percent are within one standard deviation. Any anomalies—that is, items that are more than three standard deviations from the mean—must be investigated as potential errors or fraud. A *binomial distribution* of data occurs when a series of tests are conducted with two possible answers, such as yes/no, true/false, or correct/incorrect. In accounting and auditing, this type of testing is usually conducted to determine if internal controls are effective. *Random distribution* occurs when the data does not have a discrete pattern.

Sampling Risk

Auditors should apply professional judgment in assessing sampling risk. In performing substantive tests of details, the auditor is concerned with two aspects of sampling risk:

- The *risk of incorrect acceptance* is the risk that the sample supports the conclusion that the recorded account balance is not materially misstated when it is materially misstated.
- The *risk of incorrect rejection* is the risk that the sample supports the conclusion that the recorded account balance is materially misstated when it is not materially misstated.

The auditor is also concerned with two aspects of sampling risk in performing tests of controls when sampling is used:

- The *risk of assessing control risk too low* is the risk that the assessed level of control risk based on the sample is less than the true operating effectiveness of the control.
- The *risk of assessing control risk too high* is the risk that the assessed level of control risk based on the sample is greater than the true operating effectiveness of the control.

Audit Risk Model

The audit risk model states that the audit risk is equal to the inherent risk times the control risk times the detection risk, or AR = IR × CR × DR. The inherent risk depends on the types of accounts the client has, and the control risk is determined by the auditor's evaluation of the design and the effectiveness of the client's internal controls. Again, this is an area where auditors can use data analytics to help determine the effectiveness of the controls. Many approvals, such as the approval to make a purchase or the approval to cut a check, are done in the accounting system. But the auditor can also use data analytics to tie out the invoice numbers from the PDF copies of the invoice by making sure the invoice number, the vendor name, and the amounts match so that the invoice details reflect what is on the accounting system. The auditor can run a data analytics process using AI to look at every invoice the company has and compare each to the data in the accounting system. This can reveal duplicate invoices or invoices that are not reflected in the accounting system.

Sampling

Methods appropriate for both statistical and nonstatistical sampling include *random sampling* and *systematic sampling*. In random sampling, all items have an equal chance of selection. Systematic sampling, which was commonly used before random number generators were available, selects every *n* th item with random start within the *n* interval. Methods for non-statistical sampling include the following:

- **Haphazard selection.** The auditor selects sample items without intentional bias.
- **Block selection.** This is an audit of a group of contiguous transactions, such as invoices for May, invoices in a sequence, or invoices in a date range.
- **Block amount.** Everything is audited.

With regard to sampling internal controls, it is not possible to provide absolute assurance that the internal controls are effective. Auditors cannot determine if the controls are always working, so they use hypothesis testing to test internal controls. This involves developing a hypothesis (H_0) and a null hypothesis (H_1), for example:

- H_0 – All checks are properly approved prior to being signed.
- H_1 – All checks are not approved prior to being signed.

The auditor tests the null hypothesis and if the sample doesn't have any data points supporting the null hypothesis, then the null hypothesis is rejected and the hypothesis is accepted.

¶ 606 DATA ANALYSIS

There are two basic types of analytical procedures. One is *quantitative analysis*, which is performed on numerical data such as operational data. This information might include performance data, such as the number of widgets manufactured in one month and how many widgets were defective in each batch. Accounting data, such as payments, invoices, and receipts, is another form of quantitative information. Quantitative analysis involves things that we can define using numbers.

Qualitative analysis, on the other hand, involves things other than numbers, or unstructured data. This type of analysis can be performed on the results of question-naires, such as customer, employee, or vendor surveys. Emails, text messages, con-tracts, and other such items can be qualitatively analyzed.

As mentioned earlier in this chapter, descriptive analytics allows auditors to look at past performance whereas diagnostic analytics uncovers causes. Predictive analytics allows auditors to predict the future and help an organization choose the best options for proceeding with a project.

STUDY QUESTIONS

3. The sampling method where all items have an equal chance of selection is:

    a. Random sampling

    b. Systematic sampling

    c. Haphazard selection

    d. Block selection

4. Which type of analytics is typically used when auditing past performance?

    a. Prescriptive analytics

    b. Predictive analytics

    c. Diagnostic analytics

    d. Descriptive analytics

Designing Audit Procedures for Data Analysis

In the planning stage of the audit, when designing the audit procedures for data analysis, the auditor must consider the following:

- Is the data complete? Has all the data been input into the system? Do we have all the data that the company has? Are there any contracts or payments that were not put into the accounting system?

- Is the data accurate? Does the data on the source documents match the data in the accounting system? Tracing and vouching must be built into the data analytics.

- Is data conversion necessary? For example, if one company acquired another and they are running on different accounting systems or different types of software, that data might need to be converted.

- Does the data need to be normalized? For example, dates such as 1/1/20, 1/1/2020, January 1 2020, and 1 January 20 might need to be normalized so that all reflect the same format.

- Does the data need to be cleansed? This might be the case if errors, fraud, and duplications exist.

Auditors must look for these situations to determine what to add or remove from the system when designing their audit procedures.

Data Mining

When performing data analysis, auditors can employ statistical analysis, descriptive statistics, and inferential statistics (samples). Data mining is another tool auditors can use. Data mining software uses algorithms to identify data in large databases. There are many types of algorithms. One of the more common types are classification algorithms, which allow the auditor to gather all the transactions that belong to one account. Regression algorithms can be used to determine where things should be based on past data. Auditors can use segmentation algorithms to break up transactions, such as those that are outside three standard deviations or between two and three standard deviations of the mean for testing. Association algorithms allow auditors to bring together items that are associated. Sequence analysis algorithms can look for things such as duplicate invoices, duplicate receipt numbers, missing invoice numbers, and missing check numbers.

Electronic data analysis enables auditors to do the following:

- Retrieve values
- Filter data
- Compute derived values
- Find extremes
- Sort data
- Determine ranges
- Characterize ranges
- Find anomalies and outliers
- Cluster data
- Correlate data
- Provide contextualization (relevance to the user)

Data Visualization

One of the benefits of data analytic software is the ability to use data visualization. *Data visualization* tools represent data graphically in formats such as charts, graphs, and maps to enable users to see and understand trends, outliers, and patterns in *data*. Examples of data visualization tools and common uses include the following:

- Excel spreadsheets can be used to compare revenue by month for three different years.
- Pie charts are often used to break out travel and entertainment expenses.
- Timelines can help auditors find errors or journal entries at unusual times and determine whether there is a pattern.
- Simple infographics can illustrate the separate steps in a process, such as how a company is using raw materials, or the expenses for raw materials at different steps in the process. They can also be used to show percentages.
- Flowcharts are often used to document internal controls, or to track the flow of information through the accounting system or the flow of products through a process.

    EXAMPLE: There are numerous types of data visualization tools, including bar graphs, line graphs, genograms, link analyses, fishbone diagrams, scatterplots, data trees, histograms, box plots, area graphs, time series plots, ternary plots, pictographs, stem and leaf plots, Venn diagrams, frequency distributions, Gantt charts, arc diagrams, Sankey diagrams, rose charts, alluvial diagrams, bubble clouds, spider charts, candlestick charts, waterfall charts, dendograms, radial trees, wedge stack graphs, partition graphs, hive plots, tube maps, dependency graphs, dasymetric maps, cartograms, choropleths, and proportional symbol maps

Which tool to use depends on the type of data the auditor wants to illustrate. All of these different types of data visualization tools can help auditors present data to their clients in a manner that is easy to understand.

Categories of Bias

Another issue auditors need to consider as they use data analytics—and at any point in the audit—is bias. There are two types of bias: conscious bias and unconscious (or implicit) bias, and both can affect the audit.

Conscious bias involves intentional acts and can result from family relationships, personal relationships, work relationships (with current or former employers or coworkers), financial relationships, or business relationships (e.g., with vendors or customers). These biases are the main reason for the requirement for independence in an audit. For example, if an auditor has been auditing a certain client for five or six or ten years, those past experiences will affect how he handles the audit, what he thinks of the client, and how much he trusts the client. Social, religious, or other group memberships can also cause conscious bias.

Unconscious bias stems from things an individual may not even know he or she is doing. For example, affinity bias might result when a CPA automatically trusts other CPAs. An auditor exhibiting confirmation bias might assume she is right and cannot possibly be wrong. Bounded awareness is a type of unconscious bias in which the auditor neglects to confirm data because the numbers look reasonable or acceptable. Auditors must be careful of this type of bias so they do not pass on unconfirmed information.

Priming means an auditor is influenced by other people or data, and anchoring occurs when the auditor is convinced that a number is correct and refuses to test it. An auditor with availability bias makes decisions based only on the most recent data, ignoring earlier information.

Group think, another form of unconscious bias, means we all know what the answer is; for example, we all know that internal control works. The rush to solve is a type of unconscious bias that often occurs when hurrying to meet a deadline. Negativity bias happens when an individual gives extra weight to negative data. Because an auditor found some errors, she may become overly cautious and test more.

People with ambiguity bias simply do not care. Employees who have already found another job and are getting ready to leave the company might act with this type of bias. Blind spot bias prevents auditors from recognizing issues. Less experienced employees, or those who are new to the auditing or accounting profession, might not recognize issues because they do not have the necessary training or experience.

An empathy gap occurs when people allow their emotions to control their decisions. For instance, an auditor might not want to upset a client who brings the firm a lot of revenue. Focalism means over relying on the first data collected. For example, an auditor may have noticed that there were a number of internal control issues when he tested the internal controls in the first quarter, and of course he brought those issues to the client's attention and they were corrected. But at the end of the year, he is still concentrating on those issues.

A type of unconscious bias called framing involves coming to different conclusions on the same data, depending on who presents it. Finally, the ostrich effect is simply ignoring data. An auditor might decide that because the data does not fit with the decision she has already made, she will pretend it does not exist.

Again, auditors do not exhibit these types of biased behaviors on purpose. They must be alert as to whether any unconscious biases might be affecting how they analyze a client's data.

¶ 607 BENFORD'S LAW

Benford's Law, named after physicist Frank Benford, who presented it in 1938 in a paper titled "The Law of Anomalous Numbers," is a theory that a general distribution occurs regarding the leading digits in a given data set. Many, but not all, large data sets conform to this theory. This law is one of many data tests that can be performed to identify potentially fraudulent transactions and therefore can be used in an analysis of data in an audit situation.

Benford's law states that in many naturally occurring collections of numbers, the leading significant digit is likely to be small. The formula is:

$$P(d) = \log_{10}(d + 1) - \log_{10}(d) = \log_{10}\left(\frac{d+1}{d}\right) = \log_{10}\left(1 + \frac{1}{d}\right)$$

Like any other theory, there are certain assumptions regarding the data sets to be examined with Benford's Law:

- The data must be numeric.
- The data must be randomly generated numbers:
  — Not restricted by maximums or minimums
  — Not assigned numbers
- It works best on large sets of data (populations or large samples).
- It looks at magnitudes of orders (numbers migrate up through 10, 100, 1,000, etc.)

As shown in the following chart, Benford's Law states that the numeral 1 will be the leading digit in a data set of numbers 30.1 percent of the time, 2 will be the leading digit 17.6 percent of the time, 3 will be the leading digit 12.5 percent of the time, and so on.

Benford's Law	
Leading Digit	**Percentage**
1	30.1
2	17.6
3	12.5
4	9.7
5	7.9
6	6.7
7	5.8
8	5.1
9	4.6

Auditors can use Microsoft Excel or other software to count the leading digits in a data set, chart their findings, and determine if that data set matches the Benford's Law expectations. Benford's law can also be used to determine the distribution of second, third, and fourth digits, although the calculation is usually just done on the first digit.

STUDY QUESTIONS

5. An unconscious bias where you have a tendency to get along with others that are similar to you is called:

    a. Confirmation bias

    b. Bounded awareness

    c. Affinity bias

    d. Priming

6. Under Benford's Law, the leading digit with the highest percentage is:

    a. 1

    b. 3

    c. 9

    d. There is no highest percentage, they all occur 11.1 percent of the time.

CPE NOTE: When you have completed your study and review of chapters 3-6, which comprise Module 2, you may wish to take the Final Exam for this Module. Go to **cchcpelink.com/printcpe** to take this Final Exam online.

MODULE 3: FRAUD OVERVIEW— CHAPTER 7: 2020 Fraud Review

¶ 701 WELCOME

One of the main reasons certified public accountants (CPAs) and other professionals often fail to detect fraud is that they are too honest. They find it difficult to think like a criminal. This chapter is designed for individuals who would like to refresh their understanding of fraud schemes and to learn how to recognize the red flags for detecting fraud. Understanding how criminals commit fraud is the first step in preventing fraud.

¶ 702 LEARNING OBJECTIVES

Upon completion of this chapter, you will be able to:

- Understand theories as to why people commit fraud
- Recognize fraud schemes that affect businesses and individuals
- Identify red flags for fraud
- Recognize the different types of fraud, including occupational fraud, cyber fraud, financial fraud, tax fraud, and identity theft

¶ 703 OVERVIEW OF FRAUD

First, it is important to define what fraud is. The basic definition of fraud from *Black's Law Dictionary* is:

> An intentional perversion of truth for the purpose of inducing another in reliance upon it to part with some valuable thing belonging to him or to surrender a legal right. A false representation of a matter of fact, whether by words or conduct, by false or misleading allegations, or by concealment of that which should have been disclosed, which deceives and is intended to deceive another so that he shall act upon it to his legal injury. Anything calculated to deceive, whether by a single act or combination, or by suppression of the truth, or suggestion of what is false, whether it be by direct falsehood or innuendo, by speech or silence, word of mouth, or look or gesture. A generic term, embracing all multifarious means which human ingenuity can devise, and which are resorted to by one individual to get advantage over another by false suggestions or by suppression of truth, and includes all surprise, trick, cunning, dissembling, and any unfair way by which another is cheated.

The fact that fraud is an intentional act is key. Errors happen and people make mistakes, but fraudulent acts are committed on purpose. There has to be some type of false representation, and it does not have to be verbal in nature. Fraud also includes omitting information, especially anything pertinent to or material to a transaction. So failing to give people information, hiding information, or pretending that you do not know the information are all types of fraud. For fraud to occur, somebody has to make a false statement or omission that another party relied upon to their detriment. There has to be some harm. Therefore, simply lying is not considered fraud.

Fraud Research and Theories

Researchers have developed several theories about fraud. Gabriel Tarde was a 19th-century French criminologist who developed the *theory of differential reinforcement*. The major components of this theory are that people are most likely to imitate the actions of both those with whom they are in close contact and their superiors. The concept of individuals imitating the actions of their superiors is a grounding principle in the Committee of Sponsoring Organizations' (COSO) control environment, or as it is often referred to, the "tone at the top." Ethics flows from the top of an organization down through the ranks. The theory of differential reinforcement supports an organization's need for an ethics policy and a code of conduct. Gabriel Tarde was also the first to recognize a criminal's tendency to return to the scene of the crime and to be a repeat offender.

Dr. Edwin Sutherland came up with the *theory of differential association*, which explains that criminals learn their behavior by associating with other criminals, and therefore people who do not associate with criminals do not learn how to commit crimes. Sutherland opposed incarceration except for extremely violent crimes because he theorized that putting people in prison was like sending them to a criminal university. He coined the term *white-collar criminal* for crimes involving a breach of trust rather than violence.

Dr. Ronald Akers developed the *social learning theory*, which is a combination of the differential reinforcement and differential association theories. He suggested that peer pressure can keep people from committing crime. For organizations, having internal controls, conducting anti-fraud training, and ensuring employees are aware of the consequences of fraud can help prevent them from committing crimes. When people know that they will be ostracized for committing criminal acts, they are less likely to do so. On the other hand, if an individual is part of a group in which everybody is committing crimes, he or she will be more likely to do the same. Peer pressure can be extraordinarily strong.

Dr. Donald Cressey, a student of Dr. Sutherland, created the concept of the *fraud triangle* in 1952. According to Cressey, three factors are evident when people commit fraud:

- Pressure
- Rationalization
- Opportunity

Pressure comes from the need for something, such as cash to pay bills. Rationalization is how individuals find ways to believe actions they know are wrong are acceptable under the circumstances, such as convincing themselves they are only borrowing the money rather than stealing it. Finally, opportunity occurs when the victim allows the fraudster access to the victim's assets.

Elements of Fraud

There are three basic elements of fraud:

- The act
- Concealment
- Conversion

The act consists of the actual theft or misappropriation of assets. Concealment represents the perpetrator's attempts to hide the act from others, and conversion is the process of turning the ill-gotten gains into something the perpetrator can use. Criminals can use other people's identities to conceal their illegal activities.

¶703

The elements of fraud are used by managers to help identify the risk of fraud in a business. Internal controls can be used to help prevent or detect the act, which is the first element of fraud. Managers and those with responsibility for governance must implement effective internal controls to restrict a perpetrator's access to assets and deny them the opportunity to commit the act of fraud. Based on the elements of fraud theory, managers and those charged with governance concentrate on developing internal controls for the theft or misappropriation of assets. The elements of fraud theory focus on starting with the criminal act without considering the demographics or motivations of the fraud perpetrators that led up to the act.

Fraud can cost organizations a significant amount of money. A study by the Association of Certified Fraud Examiners (ACFE) indicated that organizations lose over $7 billion a year to fraud, about $130,000 per case on average. Twenty-two percent of those cases involve losses of more than $1 million.

STUDY QUESTION

1. The social learning theory was developed by:
   a. Gabriel Tarde
   b. Ronald Akers
   c. Edwin Sutherland
   d. Donald Cressey

¶704 OCCUPATIONAL AND NON-OCCUPATIONAL FRAUDS

Frauds that affect the workplace are considered to be occupational frauds. There are three basic types of occupational frauds:

- Asset misappropriation
- Financial statement fraud
- Corruption

Asset misappropriation is the theft of either tangible or intangible assets, for example, fixed assets, inventory, or sensitive data. Financial statement fraud is commonly referred to as "cooking the books." Corruption is the misuse of an individual's position for personal gain.

According to the ACFE, asset misappropriation is the most common type of occupational fraud, followed by corruption and financial statement fraud. Many times, these types of fraud occur together because criminals commit financial statement fraud to cover up corruption and theft of assets.

A number of non-occupational frauds affect businesses as well, but they also affect individuals. Examples include the following:

- **Medical insurance fraud.** This type of fraud drives up the premiums that businesses pay for their employees for medical insurance. One example is when a policyholder puts nonrelatives on his or her policy as dependents to fraudulently obtain coverage for them.
- **Unemployment fraud.** Examples include misstating wages to qualify for a higher payout, and going back to work at a new employer while continuing to collect unemployment benefits.

- **Worker's compensation fraud.** Many people know of someone who has faked or exaggerated an injury in order to get worker's compensation.
- **Product liability fraud.** This involves hiding harmful issues related to a product.
- **Advertising fraud.** This can include false advertising, such as when a drug company promises results that do not happen.
- **Identity theft.** Someone steals the identifying information of another individual or business to use it to commit a crime. The many types of identity theft will be discussed in more detail later in this chapter.

Other types of non-occupational frauds are credit card fraud, Internet frauds, liability fraud, and employment fraud.

¶705 FRAUD RISKS AND RED FLAGS

To reduce the likelihood of fraud occurring, organizations must be aware of fraud risks. Different types of organizations face different risks. The risks for small businesses include:

- Lack of segregation of duties
- Lack of management review
- Management's limited accounting knowledge
- Minimal, if any, internal controls
- Informal atmosphere
- Related parties
- Use of QuickBooks

Government entities should be aware of the following risks:

- Lack of segregation of duties
- Lack of management review
- Elected officials' limited accounting knowledge
- Minimal, if any, internal controls
- Lack of a profit motive
- Corruption
- "Use it or lose it" budgets
- Fund accounting

Not-for-profits also face fraud risks, such as these:

- Lack of segregation of duties
- Lack of management review
- Management's limited accounting knowledge
- Minimal, if any, internal controls
- Informal atmosphere
- Related parties
- Use of volunteers
- Accounting records
- Cash transactions
- Donations of tangible and financial assets

Red Flags

Red flags can alert entities that fraud might be occurring. According to an ACFE study, in about 85 percent of fraud cases, the fraudsters displayed one or more of the major red flags. The first red flag is living beyond one's means. In other words, if somebody is making $35,000 a year, driving a brand-new Lamborghini, and living in a big mansion, this might be an indication that person is committing some type of fraud.

Employees who are having financial difficulties are another red flag. Although the majority of employees with financial problems will not cross the line and turn into criminals, a certain percentage will, if the situation is right. The 20–60–20 rule suggests that 20 percent of employees will never break the rules, no matter what; 60 percent are situational opportunists, which means if the pressure is strong and the opportunity presents itself, they may break the rules. The remaining 20 percent of employees are trying to figure out how to steal from their employer. The question is, which employee is which? Employers should be suspicious of employees who have an unusually close association with a vendor or customer. For example, if the employee goes on vacation with the vendor, or the vendor lets the employee use its private plane, these are huge red flags. Another red flag is an employee who has control issues; he doesn't want to share his duties, won't cross-train somebody on his job, or resents his supervisor attempting to check on his work. A divorce, family problems, or medical problems can also put pressure on employees to commit fraud.

Employees who have a wheeler-dealer attitude are another concern. For such employees, everything is a quid pro quo—"You scratch my back and I'll scratch yours." Wheeler-dealers find it quite easy to cross the line. In some cases, employees may fear losing their job after receiving a poor performance evaluation. The fact that they might be fired soon makes it easier for them to consider committing fraud. Some employees who are laid off actually steal from their employer on their way out the door. Cuts in pay, demotions, or even involuntary cuts in hours can cause people to react by perpetrating criminal acts.

¶ 706 COMMON FRAUD SCHEMES

Financial Statement Frauds

As mentioned earlier, financial statement fraud is one of the three types of occupational frauds. Financial statement frauds are characterized by the following:

- Manipulation, falsification, or alteration of accounting records or supporting documents from which financial statements are prepared
- Misrepresentation in or intentional omission from the financial statements of events, transactions, or other significant information
- Intentional misapplication of accounting principles relating to amounts, classification, manner of presentation, or disclosure

Improper revenue recognition includes situations where revenue is recognized before it is properly earned, revenue for long-term contracts is recognized at signing, contingent revenue is recognized, side agreements are used, revenue is recognized in the wrong period, fictitious revenue is recorded on the books, or there are fictitious customers and sales. Round tripping, bill and hold fraud, disguised consignment sales, channel stuffing, and the manipulation of customer discounts or incentives are other signs that revenue is not being recognized correctly.

Red flags for improper recognition of expenses include:

- Failure to record expenses
- Recording improper expenses
- Capitalizing expenses

- Off-the-books expenses
- Recording expenses in the wrong period
- Failure to record liabilities

Improper asset valuation may include the following:

- Improperly recording acquisition cost
- Improper depreciation or amortization
- Improper capitalization
- Failure to impair fixed assets or improper impairments
- Recording unowned assets
- Recording fictitious accounts receivable
- Extending the useful life of assets
- Manipulating inventory counts
- Consolidating entities not under the company's control
- Failure to write off unused assets
- Failure to write off uncollectible receivables
- Failure to write off obsolete inventory

Improper estimates are another way to "cook the books." An employee who makes an improper estimate might reason that she was not committing fraud; she just made a bad estimate, or an error. Therefore, auditors must review estimates to determine if they are reasonable. Things to watch for include:

- Useful life of an asset
- Repairs and warranties
- Allowance for doubtful accounts
- Percentage of completion
- Contingencies

Financial statement disclosure issues to examine include missing, fictitious, or misleading disclosures, and false information in the Management's Discussion and Analysis (MD&A).

Accounts Receivable and Cash Frauds

There are numerous types of accounts receivable and cash frauds. Some of the most common are detailed in this section.

Account identity theft. With account identity theft, the criminal sets up a bank account in a name similar to that of the victim. The criminal then steals checks intended for the victim and deposits them in the criminal's bank account. The funds are then withdrawn or wired out of the account as soon as the check clears. The payor sees that a check they wrote cleared and they are unlikely to take any action until they are contacted by the victim, usually several months later, to inquire about a past due payment.

Check swaps. Another twist on stealing checks is to swap the stolen checks with fraudulent checks or paper hanging. This is done to buy time to allow the stolen checks to clear the bank and make sure there are no discrepancies in the deposits.

Fraudulent sales. Accounts receivable can be used to help post fraudulent sales. The revenue and receivable are posted to the books. When the customer, sometimes a shell company or fake customer, doesn't pay the receivable, it is written off. This can be done by management for a better bottom line or by employees to earn bonuses or commissions.

Round tripping. Sales and accounts receivable are created and inventory transfers are reflected on the books of the two companies. Often the inventory sold never leaves the "seller's" warehouse. This is done to increase revenue at the end of a period. In the new period, the companies do a barter trade for their inventory and write off the receivables.

Re-aging receivables. In this type of fraud, a past-due receivable is paid, usually with a journal entry, and a new receivable is created with the current date. This clears the aged receivable and prevents the write-off of the receivable. Aged receivables can be re-aged multiple times to make the accounts receivable aging report show only current, and few past due, invoices.

Receivables dumping. Receivables dumping occurs when an employee, who normally has a connection with a collection company, writes off a collectible receivable and sends it out for collection. The collection company usually gets a third of the collection, and the employee either has an undisclosed interest in the collection company or is receiving a kickback from the collection company.

Unrecorded payments on bad debts. Sometimes companies receive payments on accounts that have been written off as uncollectible. The payments can come from a customer, a lawyer, or the bankruptcy courts. Since the company is not expecting to receive payments on accounts it has charged off, it is easy to divert these funds.

Skimming. Skimming is a fraud where employees or volunteers steal cash or checks before transactions are entered into the accounting system. They provide the customer with products or services, and instead of entering the transaction into the cash register, they pocket the payment and do not record a sale. This is a common fraud when employees are working alone, in drive-through retail outlets, and at fundraising events for not-for-profit organizations. Governments are also susceptible because many taxpayers prefer to pay taxes and fines in cash or by check. Skimming can be difficult to detect because nothing has been entered into the accounting system so there is no audit trail or transaction to review. Common internal controls that are effective in preventing and detecting skimming include using cameras to record cash registers and cash collection points and requiring receipts for all sales.

Skimming is also done by business owners to reduce their tax burden. By removing receipts from the business, they can reduce both their sales tax and income tax liabilities. A common red flag for owner skimming is owners offering discounts for cash payments. The owners pocket the cash payments and don't include them in the company financials or on their tax returns. This type of fraud can be difficult to detect and is usually discovered during a tax audit when the auditors do a lifestyle audit to show the business owner is living well beyond his or her means based on the reported tax income. Receipts skimming is also done to reduce alimony and child support payments, which are based on income. Another common reason for owner skimming is to qualify for government benefits or for needs-based scholarships and government-backed student loans for their children's college education.

Lapping. Lapping is a fraud scheme where employees "rob Peter to pay Paul." Lapping most commonly occurs in organizations that have many customers who have similar payments.

> **EXAMPLE:** A typical lapping plan works in the following pattern. An employee steals a payment from Customer A and pockets the money. Before Customer A gets a late notice or late fee, the employee steals a payment from Customer B and posts it to Customer A's account. Then the employee steals funds

from Customer C to cover the theft from Customer B. At this point, Customer A and Customer B are current on their payments and the employee only needs to worry about covering the payment for Customer C. It can be difficult for employees to track all the payments they have stolen and to cover them before they become past due, making lapping one of the easier frauds to detect.

Payment diversions. Payment diversions occur when an employee accepts a payment from the customer and posts it to his or her own account or to the account of a friend, relative, or other accomplice. This type of fraud can be difficult to prove as the employee will assert that he "just made a mistake."

Fraudulent coupons or discounts. Fraudulent coupons or discounts are posted on the account after the sale is complete to reduce the amount of the accounts receivable, and the amount of the fraudulent coupon or discount is stolen when the customer pays the full balance.

Factoring fraud. Factoring fraud occurs when management inflates the value of accounts receivable in order to qualify for a loan using the receivables as collateral. Fictitious sales are recorded on the books to increase the accounts receivable balance. Factoring fraud is usually done in conjunction with receivables re-aging.

Expense reimbursement frauds. Examples of this type of fraud include the following:

- Multiple employees submitting for the same expense
- Conflict of interest in purchasing
- Unauthorized expenses
- Overstated expenses
- Fictitious expenses
- Split expenses
- Duplicate receipts
- Expensing items and then selling them
- Purchasing and canceling extended warranties
- Purchasing gift cards
- Shell companies
- Double billing
- Altering receipts
- Depositing refunds

Counterfeit currency. The use of counterfeit currency is one of the oldest cash frauds and also one of the most overlooked. The majority of fake bills today are $100 bills, and the second most commonly counterfeited bill is the $20 bill. Counterfeit currency schemes can be perpetrated by customers or employees. Customers can use counterfeit currency to pay for transactions, and employees can swap counterfeit currency for real bills in their cash drawer, which leaves the employer holding the counterfeit currency. Individuals can make counterfeit currency using a color copier, or they can purchase it on the Internet.

Common internal controls to detect counterfeit currency include using black lights, counterfeit detection pens, and counterfeit detection machines. Black lights allow employees to view the color of the security threads in modern U.S. currency. Under a black light, the security thread in a $100 bill is pink, a $50 bill is yellow, a $20 bill is green, a $10 bill is orange, and a $5 bill is blue. If the color of the security thread under a black light doesn't match the denomination of the bill, then it is a counterfeit. Counterfeit detection pens are iodine-based pens that are used to detect standard wood-based paper used in copiers and printers. U.S. currency is printed on a cloth-based paper. The iodine in the counterfeit detection pen leaves a permanent black mark on wood-based paper and a temporary brown mark on cloth-based paper.

Remember, it is illegal to use or possess counterfeit U.S. currency. The simple possession of the currency is punishable with a prison term of up to 20 years. You should not attempt to deposit or pass off counterfeit currency to another company. Federal statute 18 USC Section 471 criminalizes making copies of U.S. currency unless they are much larger or much smaller than real U.S. currency (a minimum of 50 percent larger or 25 percent smaller) or unless they are "rendered in black and white," with up to 15 years in prison. Should you receive a counterfeit bill, you are required to forward it to the U.S. Secret Service.

Theft of inventory. Who can steal a business's inventory? Obviously, employees and customers can. Suppliers can steal by short-shipping the business. Some business owners steal inventory too, but they are not really stealing from themselves—they're stealing to fudge the financial statements. Organizations must be aware that just about anybody who has access to the inventory could steal it, and must ensure they have good internal controls in place to protect both tangible and intangible assets. Types of inventory fraud include the following:

- **Larceny scheme.** This scheme involves an employee who works at a cash register colluding with an outside party. The accomplice brings several items to the checkout point, including one high-priced item. The employee rings up the items but places his hand over the barcode of the high-priced item while passing it over the scanner, thus preventing it from being recorded. The accomplice then pays for the lower priced items and walks out with all of the items, including the items not recorded by the cash register. If a supervisor is watching, or even if cameras are present, this can look like a legitimate sale and no red flags are raised—until the inventory is counted, and shortages are detected.

- **False return scheme.** Another inventory fraud scheme starts with an employee removing inventory from the store or warehouse and passing it off to an accomplice. The accomplice brings the item back to the store and requests a refund. There is usually an excuse for not having an original receipt, such as "it was a gift." The employee then processes a refund by paying the accomplice and returning the stolen item to the store's inventory.

- **Building contractor scrap scheme.** In this scheme, a contractor orders items that are larger than needed. The items are then cut to size for a project. The contractor takes the scrap and sells it or uses it to remodel his home or a fix-and-flip.

- **Phantom inventory scheme.** Inventory is sold, but the items are not removed from the inventory records. Items that are not present are included in the inventory counts.

Additional examples of inventory fraud include:

- Spoilage frauds
- Obsolescence frauds
- Shell companies
- Breakage frauds
- Capitalized costs
- Double counting
- Cut-off issues

- Consignment inventory
- False purchases
- Excess orders

Cash drawer loans. In this scheme, an employee puts a personal check, which is usually postdated, into the cash drawer and removes the cash. The employee does not immediately deposit the check but keeps it in the cash drawer until payday when the check is deposited. Thus the employee provides herself with an interest-free loan until payday when the check will finally be deposited.

Cash larceny. Cash larceny is the act of stealing cash from a register, a deposit, or a safe after it has been recorded in the accounting system. It is easier to detect than skimming because the transactions were recorded on the books. Other cash frauds include removing or altering register tapes, altering cash counts, and voiding cash transactions.

Fraudulent checks. Criminals obtain the routing and account numbers for a legitimate company's accounts and then use computers and laser printers to create fraudulent checks on the accounts to make purchases.

Washed checks. Criminals use chemicals to remove ink from a check and then rewrite the check to themselves or others.

Paper hanging. This scheme includes writing checks on closed accounts or ordering checks for closed accounts in order to pass the checks.

Disappearing ink. This type of fraud involves using disappearing ink that takes a day to disappear. For example, a check is written for $9100, but the *9* in numerical amount and the *ninety* in the written amount are written in disappearing ink so the check clears the writer's account for $100.

Check kiting. Fraudsters try to use the float between multiple checking accounts to deposit checks into one account when there are no funds in the disbursement account.

Check swaps. Another twist on stealing checks is to swap the stolen checks with fraudulent checks or paper hanging. This is done to buy time to allow the stolen checks to clear the bank and make sure there are no discrepancies in the deposits.

STUDY QUESTIONS

2. Creating new receivables to pay off older receivables is an example of:
    a. Duplicate invoices
    b. Receivables dumping
    c. Re-aging
    d. Skimming

3. Taking cash before it is recorded in the accounting system is known as:
    a. Cash larceny
    b. Kiting
    c. Skimming
    d. Cash drawer loans

4. Employees commit expense reimbursement fraud by all of the following ways, *except:*

    a. Expensing items and then selling them on the Internet

    b. Purchasing and canceling extended warranties

    c. Entertaining customers

    d. Creating shell companies

5. The security thread in a $20 bill glows _____ under a black light.

    a. Blue

    b. Green

    c. Yellow

    d. Pink

6. Which of the following is a type of inventory fraud?

    a. Bill and hold

    b. Lapping

    c. Cooking the books

    d. Short shipping

Credit Card Frauds

Credit and debit card frauds can occur at any organization that accepts credit and debit transactions. With the increase in online sales, fraudulent debit and credit card transactions have also increased. Gift card fraud is also prevalent. According to a report by Statistic Brain, 40 percent of all financial fraud is related to credit cards. This amounts to a total of $5.5 billion in credit card fraud worldwide. The same report breaks this down into five types of credit card fraud:

- 37 percent is counterfeit credit cards.
- 23 percent is lost or stolen cards.
- 10 percent is "no-card" fraud, such as giving information to a non-legitimate telemarketer.
- 7 percent is cards stolen during mailing.
- 4 percent is identity theft.

Most credit and debit card fraud occurs in the United States. In fact, a 2015 research note from Barclays stated that the United States is responsible for 47 percent of the world's credit and debit card fraud despite accounting for only 24 percent of total worldwide payment card volume. U.S. credit card fraud is on the rise. About 31.8 million U.S. consumers had their credit cards breached in 2014, more than three times the number affected in 2013. Credit card fraud isn't cheap for the banks and financial institutions either. Nearly 90 percent of credit and debit card fraud victims in 2014 received replacement credit cards, costing issuers as much as $12.75 per card. Despite the risk of fraud, credit and debit card transactions have been increasing over the last decade. There are over 407 million credit cards in use in the United States alone and over 1.5 billion credit cards in use worldwide according to CreditCards.com. Additionally, approximately 1.9 billion debit cards are being used worldwide.

Credit card application fraud is done by submitting false information to the financial institution to obtain credit cards. This is often done online or through the mail. Fraudsters also take over existing credit and debit card accounts. This can be done by using stolen credit card information to make online purchases or by creating a duplicate credit or debit card to use for live purchases. Criminals can purchase a credit and debit card duplicator online for around $150. They can also purchase blank cards, including EMV cards on the Internet. A common method used by criminals is to purchase a five-dollar gift card, then use the gift card and copy the stolen information onto the gift card using the duplicator. This allows them to present the gift card with the appropriate logo on the card, instead of using a blank white card to make a purchase. Some larger credit card fraud rings actually order credit and debit card blanks that are printed with the appropriate logos and contain all the security features of the cards issued by the banks.

While many people believe the security of their credit and debit cards has increased because the banks and card issuers added EMV (Europay MasterCard and VISA) chips to the cards, this may not in fact be true. Although the EMV chips make it more difficult for criminals to skim the information on the card and create a duplicate card, criminals have developed a new fraud scheme to take advantage of the vulnerabilities of the EMV chips. These chips are RFID, and you can pay for a transaction by waving the EMV chip card over a point-of-sale transaction device designed to capture the RFID information. What most consumers don't know is that the chips in a smart card can be read at distances up to three feet away.

Criminals are aware of the new chip card's vulnerability and they use portable, battery operated, point-of-sale devices to capture the information broadcast by the smart cards and process card present transactions. They go to crowded areas such as shopping malls, sports venues, subways, buses, and other public places carrying these portable devices and have them automatically process a card present transaction for under $50, which is the federal legal limit for the amount of a fraudulent transaction that is the responsibility of the consumer. For fraudulent transactions over $50, the card issuer is responsible for the transaction. When consumers attempt to dispute these transactions, some card issuers will argue that since the card was present, and you still have possession of the card, it must be a legitimate transaction. They may even imply you just forgot about it. Several types of credit card fraud are explained below.

Identity theft. In this type of fraud, an identity thief takes over a victim's existing checking or credit card accounts. Checking accounts are the easiest to take over because all that is needed is the bank routing number and account number, both of which can be found on the front of a victim's checks.

Debit card cracking. Criminals deposit fraudulent checks in your bank account and withdraw the funds using a debit card when the bank makes the funds available, leaving the account holder on the hook for the nonsufficient funds checks.

Duplicate card fraud. As mentioned earlier, criminals use card duplicators and blank cards to make duplicates of legitimate credit, debit, and gift cards. Skimming devices are used to record the information on the magnetic strip on the back of a card.

Stolen balance transfer checks. Criminals steal credit card statements from mailboxes. Many of these statements include balance transfer checks from the card issuer. The thieves then use these checks to obtain cash or merchandise. Because these are checks, the federal $50 limit on credit cards does not apply and the victim can be responsible for the loss.

Card not present fraud. The "card not present" fraud is usually done over the Internet. The criminal has obtained someone's card number, expiration date, and other information and uses that information to make electronic purchases.

Government Contract Fraud

Government contract fraud occurs when contractors overbill the government for products provided or services performed. The Federal False Claims Act helps to recover funds stolen with this type of fraud. Another type of government contract fraud involves supplying subpar materials on a government contract to save on expenses.

Payroll Frauds

Payroll fraud schemes can be conducted by employees, an organization's accounting department, or by its owners and managers. The most basic payroll fraud scheme conducted by employees is to improperly record hours on a time sheet, thereby getting paid for hours that are not worked. Workers have been known to ask their fellow employees to "clock me out" because they need to leave early, or to ask someone to "punch me in" if they know they are going to be late. The unwritten agreement is a quid pro quo that if you help me out now, I will do the same for you in the future. This is an example of combining asset misappropriation and corruption into one fraud scheme. Another common employee fraud scheme is slow work for overtime. The employee deliberately works slowly, knowing work needs to be done by a certain deadline, and then works overtime to get the job done.

Another scheme applies to fire department, police department, and other essential service personnel. Employees usually have sick days or personal time off that they can use, and they take those days when friends who need some extra cash are on call. They get the day off and the friend gets overtime for the shift. There is an understanding that the favor will be returned when the employee who took the day off needs some overtime. Paperwork requirements can also be used to create overtime. One example is leaving all the paperwork until the end of the shift and then working overtime to get caught up. Audits of government entities show many first responders receive half of their W-2 income from overtime. This is a difficult area to control because the work needs to be done and many times there are legitimate reasons for the overtime.

Many payroll frauds can be conducted by employees in the accounting department. Accounting personnel can enter ghost employees or ghost independent contractors into the accounting system. Accounting personnel can also give unapproved raises to related employees or sometimes give an employee an unapproved raise and then split the raise with the employee by getting a kickback every payday. Red flags for ghost employees include no deductions for insurance or retirement accounts, no use of sick time or vacation time, and multiple direct deposits being made to one account.

Managers and owners can also commit payroll fraud. Owners can misclassify employees as independent contractors in order to avoid paying payroll taxes on the employee's wages. Non-exempt employees can also be misclassified as exempt employees in order to avoid paying overtime. Some business owners and managers hire undocumented immigrants to work in their businesses because they can pay them off the books, usually in cash, and pay them less than the legally mandated federal minimum wage.

Tax Frauds

People commit tax fraud for many reasons, including greed, because they don't agree with government spending, because they don't agree with government policies, because they don't believe in paying taxes, or simply because "everyone else is doing it." There are numerous types of tax frauds available to criminals willing to break the law. Some of the more common types include income tax fraud, sales and use tax fraud, excise tax fraud, payroll tax fraud, property tax fraud, and estate and gift tax fraud.

Income tax fraud is unfortunately fairly common. It is usually done in conjunction with financial statement fraud. When most people first think of financial statement fraud, they think of large companies like Enron and WorldCom, and individuals like Bernie Madoff, who cooked the books to increase revenue and/or decrease expenses to make the company look more profitable and drive up the stock price. However, the vast number of financial statement frauds in the United States work in the opposite direction. Small and midsized businesses reduce revenue and inflate expenses in order to make the company look less profitable, thereby reducing the tax burden on the business owners. This is particularly common for sole proprietorships and pass-through entities. The ultimate goal is to reduce the income and sales taxes paid by the owners to allow them to keep more money in their pockets. Business owners do this by skimming revenue out of the business. They might even offer customers discounts for paying in cash so they don't have to record the transaction on the books or deposit the funds in a bank, which leaves a paper trail. Business owners can also record personal expenses as business expenses to reduce the taxable income of the business. The new ultra-HD TV for the house is recorded as a computer monitor for the business, or the family vacation is recorded as a business trip.

Not recording sales in the accounting system also allows the business owner to avoid paying sales and use taxes on those transactions. Business owners can also misuse their sales tax exemption certificates, which allow the business to avoid paying sales taxes on items the business purchases for resale in the business, to make personal purchases. This is commonly done in restaurants, where the owners purchase the family groceries at a restaurant supply store and use the business's sales tax exemption certificate to avoid paying sales taxes on those purchases. Many businesses make purchases on the Internet or from out of state and fail to report and pay the use taxes on those transactions. (Subsequent update - the *South Dakota versus Wayfair* decision closed some of these opportunities)

Business owners have been known to borrow money from payroll withholdings, including an employee's payroll tax withholdings, 401(k) withholdings, or other items withheld from the employee's paycheck. These monies are often used to fund operations or to pay the owners. Businesses sometimes misclassify employees as independent contractors in order to avoid paying the business's half of the employees' payroll taxes.

Additionally, failure to report tips, or to under-report tips, is another type of tax fraud. Employees believe it is harmless and that they have a low chance of getting caught. Historically that may have been correct, but with data analytics software, it is possible to compare tips that were paid by credit card or check, to transactions paid in cash. If there is a material discrepancy, the taxing authority can assess taxes on those tips as under-reported income. The IRS can also assess the business for failure to collect and remit payroll taxes on the tips.

New Generation of Cyber Frauds

Cybercrime is evolving and becoming more sophisticated. Cybercriminals now have their own social networks and even have escrow services to protect their identities and interests when conducting online transactions with other criminals. Malware XE "Malware" can be licensed by criminals, and if they experience issues, there are even tech support teams to assist them with their criminal activities. Criminals can rent botnets by the day or by the hour to use in their illicit schemes. There are also pay-for-play malware programs available for purchase on the dark web in addition to an active market for zero-day exploits.

EXAMPLE OF EXPLOITS: "Meltdown" (CVE-2017-5754) is a flaw that lets ordinary applications cross the security boundaries enforced at chip level to protect access to the private contents of kernel memory in Intel chips produced over the last decade.

"Spectre" (CVE-2017-5753 and CVE-2017-5715) is more insidious and widespread, having been found in chips from AMD and ARM as well as Intel. Spectre could enable an attacker to bypass isolation among different applications.

Phishing. Phishing is a cybercrime in which criminals contact the victim through email messages that appear to come from legitimate business or government sources. Social networking through phishing schemes is a common way to get around an organization's IT security. Often, the email headers are spoofed to make them look legitimate. One purpose of the phishing email is to obtain information such as names, addresses, Social Security numbers, phone numbers, dates of birth, credit card numbers, employer identification numbers (EINs), and other personal information from the victims. When the victims supply the information, the criminals use it to steal the victim's identity and assets. Criminals also send phishing emails containing links with the hope that the victim will click on the link and download the criminal's malware onto the victim's computer.

Criminals will often try to make you think a phishing email is coming from your bank, credit card company, or other financial institution. They may indicate there is a problem with your account or that your password is expiring. Either way, they ask you to click on the link in the email and enter your user ID and password. Once they have that information, they can use your user ID and password to access your real accounts and misappropriate all of your funds.

Criminals also use phishing emails to try to convince you there is an issue with your social media accounts, or that your accounts need to be updated. They will stress the fact that you will lose all your posts on Facebook, Twitter, LinkedIn, etc., if you don't immediately log in through the link in the email and update your account. Some criminals do their research before sending out a phishing email. This is known as *spear phishing*. They gather information on the prospective victim and tailor a phishing email directly to them. These emails can include the victim's name and the names of people the victim knows.

Vishing. Vishing is similar to phishing, but it occurs over the phone rather than over the Internet. Criminals will call a new employee or newly promoted employee (they get the information from social media) pretending to be from the IT department, and tell the employee they need to finish setting up their computer for the access they will need. The criminals tell the employee they need to remote into their computer, and then once inside the system, set up a backdoor so they have continued access to the company's computer systems.

Vishing calls are also made to alert individuals or businesses that fraud has been detected on their credit cards. The criminals use spoofed phone numbers to make it appear that the call is coming from a bank or financial institution. The criminals then ask the victim to verify information on the credit card, such as the account number, billing zip code, security code, or expiration date, in order to gain access to information that will allow them to use the credit card.

Other common vishing calls include calls that claim to be from the IRS trying to collect past due taxes, calls from collection agencies trying to collect past-due bills, and calls from law enforcement or regulatory agencies trying to collect fines. A red flag for vishing calls is a request that payment be made with gift cards, with virtual currencies, or by sending money through a money transfer service. They will also stress the urgency to pay immediately in order to avoid jail time or other penalties.

Smishing. Smishing is similar to phishing and vishing, but it is done using text messages rather than phone calls or email. Criminals try to obtain information or try to load malware on the victim's computer or mobile device.

Denial of service attacks. Denial of service (DoS) attacks occur when criminals use their own hijacked computer networks, or botnets (networks of infected computers), to bring down a website or computer system by overloading its capabilities, thereby crashing the system. In many instances, the criminals follow up on the DoS attack with an attempt to hack into the system and upload malware onto the victim's computer while the victim is busy trying to fix the damage being done by the DoS attack.

The most common type of DoS attack occurs when an attacker "floods" a network or website with large amounts of information or requests for access. The server can only process a certain number of requests at once, so if an attacker overloads the server with requests, it can't process the requests and the server crashes. This is a "denial of service" because the site cannot be accessed while it is down. Criminals will use this opportunity, while the IT team is recovering the system, to try to place malware on the system or to conduct a data breach.

Brand hacking. This cybercrime occurs when criminals post false or misleading information about a company or a product on the Internet. This is usually done via social media, and the sole purpose of the posts is to damage the reputation of the brand being hacked.

Pharming. In pharming, a virus or malicious software is secretly loaded onto the victim's computer and hijacks the web browser. When the victim types in the address of a legitimate website, he or she is rerouted to a fictitious copy of the website without realizing it.

Spoofing. Spoofing is a term used to describe activity that makes a fraudulent website or email look legitimate. Criminals can also spoof phone numbers and social media accounts. The purpose of spoofing is to make the victim believe they are communicating with someone they know, when in fact they are providing information to the criminals.

The CEO invoice spoof is a common type of email spoofing fraud directed at companies. The typical CEO email spoof occurs when criminals send an email to an accounting clerk, bookkeeper, or payables manager that appears to have originated from the CEO, CFO, or other senior executive of the company. There is usually an invoice attached with instructions to wire or ACH the funds to the vendor as soon as possible. The instructions have a tone of urgency to spur the employee into processing the transaction quickly. The bank account receiving the funds is usually overseas, or, if it is in the United States, the funds are immediately transferred overseas when they are deposited. Another version of this cybercrime requires the request for copies of payroll records or W-2 and other tax records, giving the criminals access to the personal information of the company's employees. In 2018, for the 2017 tax season, there were a large number of spoofing emails that appeared to come from a company's auditors requesting payroll information and claiming the information was needed to complete the audit.

Malware. Virtually everyone has heard of hacking. Hacking is commonly done by placing malware on a computer system in order to allow criminals to gain control of the victim's computer or gain access to information stored on the computer or other electronic device. Hacking is usually done over the Internet; any device connected to the Internet with either a wired or wireless connection is at risk of being hacked. Computers, cell phones, tablets, webcams, IoT devices, and other electronic equipment connected to the Internet are the main targets of cybercriminals. As the world is becoming more automated, cybercriminals are increasingly attacking robots and automated production systems in addition to computer information systems.

A common tool used by cybercriminals in a computer hack is a computer virus, which is a segment of computer code that attaches itself to a program, such as Microsoft Office, that is already loaded on the victim's computer. A computer virus can cause the infected program to delete, email, or copy files on the computer or to perform other actions such as altering files or destroying data. The virus creates copies of itself that it inserts in data files, so that when employees share files, they also share the computer virus. This enables the virus to spread throughout the company's system and to customers, vendors, and others with whom files have been shared.

Another common type of malware is known as a Trojan or Trojan Horse. A Trojan is a stand-alone malware program that is disguised as something else, usually a program or application that the user wanted, such as a computer game. Trojans, unlike viruses, are stand-alone programs and do not need to infect a program already installed on the computer but instead act on their own. Typical types of trojans include spyware, keystroke loggers, and other software designed to compromise a system or to gather data from a system. Malware can also be used to make an individual device or system part of a botnet. A common use is to infect computers to create a network of slave computers that is then used to mine cryptocurrencies like Bitcoin. Trojans are often disguised by piggy-backing on them on a free program or application downloaded by the unsuspecting user of the device.

A computer worm is a type of malware that transmits itself over networks and the Internet and infects any computer connecting with an infected source such as an infected website. Computer worms can be transferred by linking to or visiting infected websites. A computer worm is a stand-alone program that does not need to attach itself to an existing program on the computer. It can carry a payload, such as a ransomware program. The most common payload is a program that installs a backdoor on the infected computer.

A rootkit is specifically designed to modify the operating system of an infected computer. Legitimate uses for rootkits include installing updates and patches to a computer's operating system. However, criminals use rootkit programs to hide other malware from the user of the computer. Because a rootkit program has administrator access, it is not only able to modify the operating system but can also modify any other software installed on the computer. Rootkits can be used to hide malware that criminals placed on a victim's computers, so the victim can't find or remove the malware. Often the only fix is to wipe the computer and reload everything from a backup.

An extremely dangerous type of malware is known as a backdoor. A backdoor allows the cybercriminal unimpeded access to the infected computer, allowing the criminal to bypass the normal authentication processes. A backdoor usually provides the hacker with administrative access to the infected computer. It is the equivalent of the criminal having their own user ID and password to gain access to the system whenever they want.

An organization's employees are the weakest link in its cybersecurity defenses. The hackers know this and attack employees with phishing and vishing attacks, or by friending them on social media websites and then sending them infected links.

Ransomware. The FBI estimates that ransomware is a $1 billion a year fraud. Ransomware is a type of malware that is placed on a computer and then encrypts all of the files on the computer. Criminals then require that the victim pay a ransom in order to obtain the decryption key and have access to their files. The most well-known example of ransomware is CryptoLocker. Cryptowall 2.0 is a newer version of ransomware being used by cybercriminals. A new type of ransomware called Reveton installs itself onto the computer without the user's knowledge. Then, the computer freezes. A bogus message from the FBI pops up on the screen, saying the user violated federal law. To unlock their computer, the user must make a payment to the criminals.

For a single computer, cybercriminals will initially request a ransom ranging from $300 to $500. Larger ransoms are demanded when more computers are infected with the ransomware. Once the deadline for the payment has passed, the criminals raise the ransom demand to around $1000 per infected computer. Unfortunately, criminals are not always honest. When a victim makes a payment, sometimes the criminal gives them the decryption code, sometimes the criminal asks for more money, and sometimes the decryption code doesn't work and they refer the victim to a 900 number help desk where the victim pays by the minute for help decrypting his information. Governments have also been victims of ransomware. For example, in the spring of 2018, the City of Atlanta was infected with ransomware that shut down city services for weeks.

Typical ransomware software uses RSA 2048 encryption to encrypt files. To illustrate how strong this is, an average desktop computer is estimated to take around 6.4 quadrillion years to crack an RSA 2048 key. One issue with ransomware is that it is a franchise-type criminal activity. Criminals with no programing experience can contact ransomware developers on the dark web. The criminals pay an initial fee to get access to the ransomware, and the developer provides them with a link to send to all of their contacts. If victims click on the link, infect their systems with ransomware, and pay the ransom, the criminal gets 80 percent of the ransom and the developer gets 20 percent.

STUDY QUESTION

---

7. Which of the following cyber frauds encrypts the data on your computer?

    a. Phishing

    b. Ransomware

    c. Spoofing

    d. Spyware

Data breaches. The theft of information, also known as a data breach, is a crime that was virtually unknown two decades ago but is flourishing today. A data breach is defined as the theft of personal information including names, Social Security numbers, birth dates, medical information, driver's license numbers, user names and passwords, and financial account information such as credit or debit card numbers.

With an ever-increasing reliance on computers and information technology, organizations are increasingly susceptible to this type of fraud. Information thieves are misappropriating data and selling the stolen information on the dark web. A breach can occur because of a lack of security, the bypassing of security, or the elimination of security. Data breaches occur when information is stolen from computers and other electronic devices, or when devices containing information are lost or misplaced. Because an organization is considered to be negligent in its duties to safeguard the information provided to it by employees, customers, and others, there is a significant cost to being a victim of a data breach. Criminals breach the IT security of companies, not-for-profit organizations, and even governmental units and steal information from their computers. Often, the human resources department of an entity is targeted for payroll information, which includes Social Security numbers. Retail outlets are also targeted because they store customer information, including credit card numbers, on their computers. Not all data breaches are aimed at large organizations. Small businesses are also targeted, including tax providers, attorneys, medical offices, and insurance agents, because these professionals often have their clients' personal information stored on their computers.

One of the main reasons for stealing data is to profit from the data breach. Criminals can sell stolen user IDs and passwords for $5 to $20 each on the dark web.

Criminals are aware that many people use the same passwords for multiple websites and computer systems. The purchased IDs and passwords are input into software that searches the Internet for websites where the stolen IDs and passwords work and then notifies a human operator that access has been gained so they can determine if there is any value in the website that was illegally accessed. This is known as credential stuffing. Another large market for information on the dark web is the sale of stolen credit card numbers.

In addition to credit card, debit card, and Social Security numbers, criminals also purchase names, addresses, dates of birth, phone numbers, driver's license numbers, health insurance ID numbers, union numbers, and other personal identifying information on the dark web. These purchases are usually done with virtual currencies, such as Bitcoin. There are even resources on the Internet for up-and-coming criminals, including books and videos on how to profit from stolen credit cards and how to do credential cramming.

Over the years, the theft of data has become a very profitable crime. In today's economy, businesses offer goods and services on credit to strangers based on the data in the buyer's credit history or through electronic means of payment such as credit and debit cards. With telecommunications and Internet technology, buyers and sellers do not need to meet in person to consummate their transaction. The Internet has made access to information almost instantaneous. Additionally, people's willingness to share personal information about themselves on social media has increased the risk of that information being misappropriated. Increased access to data on the Internet has given criminals easier access to personal information from both inside and outside the United States. Identity thieves can use the Internet to gather an individual's identifying information without ever coming into personal contact with the victim.

Industries experiencing the highest costs due to data breaches include:

* Health care
* Financial
* Services
* Life science
* Industrial
* Technology
* Education
* Transportation
* Communications
* Energy
* Consumer
* Retail
* Hospitality
* Entertainment

According to the "2017 Cost of Data Breach Study" sponsored by IBM and conducted by Ponemon Institute LLC:

* The average cost of a data breach in the U.S. in 2016 was $7.35 million.
* The cost is up 15 percent since 2015.
* Smaller data breaches with less than 10,000 records stolen cost an average of $4.5 million.

¶706

- Larger data breaches with more than 50,000 records stolen cost an average of $10.3 million.
- Note that the study only looked at data breaches where fewer than 100,000 records were stolen.

Retail outlets are targets of data breaches because they store customer information, including credit and debit card numbers, on their computers. One of the most well-known data breaches occurred in 2013, and the victim was Target. It was estimated that 70 million debit and credit card numbers were stolen from Target's computers. In addition to the debit and credit card numbers, the criminals also misappropriated the customer's PINs, CVV codes, zip codes and other personal information. The initial estimates of the costs to Target for this data breach were $3.6 billion.

In September 2017, Equifax experienced a data breach in which an estimated 147 million consumers were affected. Thieves stole people's personal information contained in Equifax credit reports. The company responded by offering free credit freezes. Equifax's chief information officer, Jun Ying, was charged with insider trading for selling $1 million in stock after the breach was discovered but before the information was publicly disclosed. Other high-profile victims of data breaches include Home Depot, Chase Bank, Adobe, and Ashley Madison.

The courts have determined that companies have strict liability for lost information. In other words, the victims do not need to prove the stolen information was used in an identity theft. The fact that they need to pay to monitor their credit or take other actions to protect their identity creates sufficient grounds for damage awards. Therefore, businesses must use reasonable procedures to secure data in their possession. The procedures must be documented in writing and be tested or audited on periodically. There is no way to guarantee that an organization will not become a victim of a data breach, but good internal controls can reduce the risk of becoming a victim of this type of fraud.

Personal information obtained in a data breach can be used to commit many forms of fraud and identity theft, including the following:

- **Criminal identity theft.** This occurs when the perpetrator, who is using a stolen identity, is arrested for a crime. The perpetrator uses victims' identities to open businesses and bank accounts and then process stolen checks and credit cards through these accounts. Most individuals don't find out about this type of identity theft until they are arrested for crimes they didn't commit.
- **Medical identity theft.** A fraudster uses the victim's medical insurance. As a result, the victim could find that he or she is uninsurable.
- **Insurance identity theft.** Types of insurance affected by this fraud include auto insurance, homeowners insurance, life insurance, business insurance, malpractice insurance, and errors and omissions (E&O) insurance.
- **Child identity theft.** A child identity thief steals the identity of a person under legal age. Often, children don't find out about their identity being stolen until they are older and apply for student loans or attempt to get a job.
- **Professional identity theft.** In this type of theft, a fraudster steals the professional identity of another person. Because professional licenses and license numbers are a matter of public record, it is relatively easy to commit this type of identity theft.
- **Business identity theft.** Thieves use a business's name to obtain loans or credit. This crime is usually committed by insiders or current or former employees who had access to the business's financial information. It often involves the use of spoofed or fraudulent websites to obtain personal information from victims.

- **New account fraud.** Thieves use a victim's personal information (including Social Security number) to open new financial accounts.

- **Account takeover fraud.** In this type of fraud, an identity thief takes over a victim's existing account. Checking accounts are the easiest to take over. All that is needed is the bank routing number and account number, both of which can be found on the front of a victim's checks.

- **Credential stuffing.** One of the main reasons for stealing data is to profit from the data breach. Criminals can sell stolen user IDs and passwords on the dark web. They are aware that many people use the same passwords for multiple websites and computer systems. The purchased IDs and passwords are input into software that searches the Internet for websites where the stolen IDs and passwords work and then notifies a human operator that access has been gained so they can determine if there is any value in the website that was illegally accessed.

- **Identity cloning.** This crime includes multiple forms of identity theft. Individuals who are attempting to evade child support or creditors, running from the law, or otherwise attempting to conceal their true identity clone the identity of the victim and use it openly in plain sight.

- **Synthetic identity theft.** In this type of identity theft, the perpetrator creates a fabricated identity, usually online. Catfishing often involves using a real Social Security number that is then linked to the fabricated identity.

- **Government benefits fraud.** A fraudster applies for government benefits, such as Social Security or Medicare, in the name of the victim. Perpetrators of this fraud also include individuals who continue to apply for and receive government benefits for deceased individuals.

- **Government documents fraud.** In this type of fraud, a criminal obtains government documents, such as a driver's license, Medicare card, Social Security card, or other document. The documents have the name of the victim, but usually have the fraudster's photo.

- **Employment fraud.** In this scheme, a fraudster uses the victim's name and Social Security number to obtain employment. Often, this crime is committed because the perpetrator of the fraud is in the country illegally and needs legitimate documentation to obtain employment.

- **Utility fraud.** A criminal uses a victim's personal information to open accounts with electric, gas, cable, phone, or other utility companies. Bills are often sent to a fictitious address and left unpaid.

- **Stolen identity refund fraud.** Tax refund identity fraud, which is also known as stolen identity refund fraud, occurs when a criminal uses an individual's personal information to submit fraudulent information to the IRS. There are multiple ways this can be done. The most common type of tax return refund fraud involves obtaining the victim's name, address, and Social Security number and filing fraudulent tax returns in order to receive refunds from the IRS. The income and other information submitted with the return is usually made up by the criminals in order to maximize the refunds they receive. Usually, the victims find out about this type of identity theft when they go to file their tax returns and the IRS notifies them that they already filed a return for that year.

STUDY QUESTIONS

8. A data breach occurs when:

   a. Information is electronically copied from a credit card by a waiter at a restaurant.

   b. A fraudster takes a picture of a credit card while standing in line.

   c. Information is stolen from a company computer.

   d. A shell company is used to process transactions on stolen credit cards.

9. Which of the following frauds involves opening bank accounts using false information?

   a. Cash drawer loans

   b. Skimming

   c. Criminal identity theft

   d. Refund frauds

10. A fraudster using the professional license of another person would be considered:

   a. Business identity theft

   b. Financial identity theft

   c. Professional identity theft

   d. Employment identity theft

11. Which type of cyber fraud involves using stolen user IDs and passwords to try to access multiple IT systems?

   a. Data breach

   b. Credential stuffing

   c. Ransomware

   d. Phishing

¶ 707 OTHER TYPES OF FRAUD

Money Laundering

Money laundering often coexists with fraud and other criminal activities. When criminals steal money, they have to launder the money to bring it back into the mainstream so they can spend the funds without any questions being asked. The term *money laundering* originated when Al Capone was using legitimate businesses, which were in fact laundromats, to make cash deposits of his illegally obtained funds into Chicago banks. The three basic steps for laundering money are:

- **Placement.** The initial deposit of the funds into an account at a financial institution.

- **Layering.** Moving the funds through various businesses entities, such as trusts, limited liability companies, not-for-profits, and corporations, and often through multiple countries to hide the origins of the funds.

- **Integration.** Moving the funds into a legitimate account controlled by the money launderer to make the funds appear legitimate.

The U.S. Department of the Treasury estimates that more than $300 billion in illicit funds is generated from money laundering on an annual basis. Fraud and drug trafficking generate a majority of these illicit funds. Money laundering schemes are often perpetrated by cash-based businesses, such as bars, restaurants, laundries, and clubs.

Corruption

Corruption occurs when individuals use their position in their company, with a not-for-profit, or with a governmental entity for their own personal gain. Anyone in a position of power can be tempted to cross the line. Corruption involves unethical behavior by those in positions of power. It can be as simple as dishonesty, or it can be an elaborate fraud scheme. The basic tenet of corruption is that the individual is doing it for personal gain. Corruption has been uncovered in politics, associations, sports, academics, unions, governments, not-for-profits, and businesses. Corruption is more likely to occur in larger organizations of more than 100 employees. Small organizations are not free from the risk of corruption; they just have a lower risk.

For corruption to occur, the Four P's—power, preference, payments, and privilege—must be present. Someone has to have the power to make or influence a decision. They have to exercise that power to provide preferential treatment based on their relationship, or on receiving something of value, and there has to be a beneficiary of that preference.

Many people consider corruption to include a monetary payment, but money isn't the only thing that can be used to influence people. Debt forgiveness, loans, sexual favors, access to decision-makers, keeping secrets, and the free or discounted use of assets are all examples of methods of payments used in corruption schemes. The following are just some of the forms corruption can take.

Petty corruption. This type of corruption involves the exchange of small gifts or the use of personal property or connections in exchange for favors, or for speedy approvals from governments.

Bribery. Bribery is the paying or receiving of something of value (it doesn't have to be money) in exchange for preferential treatment or special favors. Kickbacks and bid rigging are two examples of bribery.

Illegal gratuities. An illegal gratuity occurs when someone provides a gift, or something of value, after favorable actions have been completed. Unlike a bribe, an illegal gratuity isn't usually arranged in advance of the action, and you don't have to prove an intent to influence the person who received the gift.

Extortion and blackmail. Extortion and blackmail are other examples of corrupt behavior. In these types of fraud, someone is threatened with actions, such as violence against themselves or their loved ones, or is threatened with the release or publication of information that could harm the person's reputation.

Abuse of discretion. Abuse of discretion occurs when an individual misuses his or her power or authority for personal gain; for example, a board member who favors a vendor owned by a friend presses the company to select that vendor. Other abuses of authority include favoritism, cronyism, and nepotism when people in positions of authority provide special treatment or favors to friends, associates, or family members.

Conflicts of interest. A conflict of interest impairs an individual's ability to make a fair and impartial decision. These conflicts usually result in the person acting to benefit themselves instead of meeting their fiduciary responsibilities to the organization or individuals they are representing.

Graft. Graft is the use of a political office, either an elected or appointed position, for personal gain. Taking a position on a political issue in exchange for campaign contributions is one example of graft. Accepting an all-expenses-paid vacation in exchange for voting a certain way is another example.

STUDY QUESTION

12. Which of the following is one of the three steps of money laundering?
  a. Layering
  b. Opportunity
  c. Conversion
  d. Rationalization

¶ 708 CONSEQUENCES OF COMMITTING FRAUD

According to the ACFE's "2018 Report to the Nation on Occupational Fraud and Abuse," over the past 10 years, occupational fraud referrals to prosecution have declined by 16 percent. The top reason companies give for not prosecuting people who committed fraud is they don't want bad publicity. Organizations don't want the fraud reported in the news or on the Internet; they don't want their name to be tied to fraudulent activity.

Typically, the only negative effect a fraudster experiences for committing fraud is termination from employment. In fact, in six percent of fraud cases, the perpetrator receives no punishment at all for committing fraud. Sometimes perpetrators sign a settlement agreement, but they do not always make the prescribed payments. In other cases, by the time an organization discovers the fraud, the person who committed it is no longer employed there. Often, once a perpetrator learns that a fraud investigation has been begun, he or she abruptly leaves the company.

Of the perpetrators who have been caught, only 4 percent had a prior conviction for fraud. It is exceedingly difficult to convict people for fraud because the organization has to prove intent. In a majority (53 percent) of fraud cases, the victims of fraud recovered nothing. Victims received a partial recovery in 32 percent of cases and recovered all their losses only 15 percent of the time. The smaller the fraud, the more likely victims are to recover. It is interesting to note that most of the recovery is obtained through insurance claims rather than from the criminals who perpetrated the fraud.

CPE NOTE: When you have completed your study and review of chapter 7, which comprises Module 3, you may wish to take the Final Exam for this Module. Go to **cchcpelink.com/printcpe** to take this Final Exam online.

¶ 10,100 Answers to Study Questions

¶ 10,101 MODULE 1—CHAPTER 1

1. a. *Correct.* **As a result of the release of ASU 2016-02, the previous lease accounting standards prescribed within ASC 840 were superseded, with the new lease standards included within ASC 842.**

b. *Incorrect.* ASC 845 relates to the accounting for nonmonetary transactions. While the issuance of the new lease standards through ASU 2016-02 did make certain conforming amendments to ASC 845, the topic was not superseded. These conforming amendments can be found within Section B of the ASU 2016-02.

c. *Incorrect.* ASC 605 relates to revenue recognition. The release of the new leasing standard did not supersede requirements within this topic.

d. *Incorrect.* ASC 250 relates to the accounting for accounting changes and error corrections. The release of the new leasing standard did not include any amendments to this topic.

2. a. *Incorrect.* Whether the customer has rights to operate the asset is not the first determination to be made when determining if a contract contains a lease. However, this is an important consideration that must be assessed when concluding whether a contract does in fact contain a lease.

b. *Incorrect.* Whether the customer designed the asset is not the first determination to be made when determining if a contract contains a lease. However, this is an important consideration that must be assessed when concluding whether a contract does in fact contain a lease.

c. *Correct.* **Whether there is an identified asset is the first determination to be made when determining if a contract contains a lease. It is important to note that identification of an asset within a contract can be made either explicitly or implicitly.**

d. *Incorrect.* Whether the customer obtains substantially all of the economic benefits is not the first determination to be made when determining if a contract contains a lease. However, this is an important consideration that must be assessed when concluding whether a contract does in fact contain a lease.

3. a. *Incorrect.* To provide additional clarity on this topic, the FASB published a Q&A that addressed some of the complexities related to these lease concessions and how companies are expected to apply the lease modifications guidance.

b. *Incorrect.* The SEC did not publish a specific Q&A regarding COVID-19 impacts to lease modifications. Instead, the FASB published a Q&A that addressed some of the complexities related to these lease concessions and how companies are expected to apply the lease modifications guidance.

c. *Incorrect.* Based on the FASB's Q&A released, an entity should provide disclosures about material concessions granted or received and the accounting effects.

d. *Correct.* **If a lease modification is not accounted for as a separate contract, then a company is required to reassess the classification of the lease as of the effective date of the modification based on the modified terms and conditions.**

4. a. *Incorrect.* If an entity estimates expected credit losses using a discounted cash flow method, the entity should not discount expected cash flows using the weighted average cost of capital. This is the rate that a company is expected to pay on average to all its security holders to finance its assets.

b. *Correct.* **If an entity estimates expected credit losses using a discounted cash flow method, the entity should discount expected cash flows using the effective interest rate. Furthermore, when a discounted cash flow method is applied, the allowance for credit losses should reflect the difference between the amortized cost basis and the present value of the expected cash flows.**

c. *Incorrect.* If an entity estimates expected credit losses using a discounted cash flow method, the entity should not discount expected cash flows using the LIBOR rate. This is a benchmark rate that some of the world's leading banks charge each other for short-term loans.

d. *Incorrect.* If an entity estimates expected credit losses using a discounted cash flow method, the entity should not discount expected cash flows using the cost of equity. The cost of equity is the return (often expressed as a rate of return) a firm theoretically pays to its equity investors (i.e., shareholders) to compensate for the risk they undertake by investing their capital.

5. a. *Correct.* **This is one of the categories of financial statement disclosures for available-for-sale debt securities. For certain of these disclosures requiring presentation in tabular form, these should be disaggregated by those investments that have been in a continuous unrealized loss position for less than 12 months and those that have been in a continuous unrealized loss position for 12 months or longer.**

b. *Incorrect.* Disclosures with respect to past-due status relate to assets measured at amortized costs. Specifically, an entity is required to provide an aging analysis of the amortized cost basis for financial assets that are past due as of the reporting date, disaggregated by class of financing receivable and major security type.

c. *Incorrect.* Disclosures with respect to nonaccrual status relate to assets measured at amortized costs. Entities are required to disclose nonaccrual policies, including the policies for discontinuing accrual of interest, recording payments received on nonaccrual assets (including the cost recovery method, cash basis method, or some combination of those methods), and resuming accrual of interest, if applicable.

d. *Incorrect.* Disclosures with respect to collateral-dependent financial assets relate to assets measured at amortized costs. For a financial asset for which the repayment is expected to be provided substantially through the operation or sale of the collateral and the borrower is experiencing financial difficulty, an entity should identify the type of collateral and a qualitative description of the extent to which collateral secures its collateral-dependent financial assets.

6. a. *Incorrect.* For public business entities that are U.S. SEC filers, the amendments are effective for fiscal years beginning after December 15, 2019, including interim periods within those fiscal years. As a result, the new credit losses standard is effective in January 2020 for U.S. SEC filers.

b. *Incorrect.* This was the original effective date for the new credit losses standard for private companies. However, this effective date was delayed to provide these entities additional time for implementation.

c. *Incorrect.* Originally, the new credit losses standard was set to be adopted by smaller reporting entities and other private entities generally one or two years after public business entities. However, in October 2019, the FASB approved its August 2019 proposal to grant private companies, not-for-profit organizations, and certain small public companies various effective date delays on its credit losses standards.

d. *Correct.* **All other public business entities that are not SEC filers, as well as private entities and all others, are now required to adopt the new standard in January 2023 (instead of January 2021).**

¶ 10,102 MODULE 1—CHAPTER 2

1. a. *Incorrect.* This is not the first step in the new revenue recognition model; it is the second step. The FASB ASC Master Glossary defines the term *performance obligation* as a promise in a contract with a customer to transfer the customer either a good or service that is distinct or a series of distinct goods or services that are substantially the same and that have the same pattern of transfer to the customer.

b. *Incorrect.* This is not the first step in the new revenue recognition model; it is the third step. The FASB defines the term *transaction price* within the ASC Master Glossary as the amount of consideration to which an entity expects to be entitled to in exchange for transferring promised goods or services to a customer, excluding amounts collected on behalf of third parties. Within the Board's BCs, it is noted that the objective in determining the transaction price at the end of each reporting period is to predict the total amount of consideration to which the entity will be entitled from the contract.

c. *Correct.* **This is the first step in the new revenue recognition model. While this step may seem fairly straightforward, the FASB included additional criteria within this step that must be met before an entity would apply the revenue recognition model. The additional criteria are largely derived from previous revenue recognition guidance and other existing standards.**

d. *Incorrect.* This is not the first step in the new revenue recognition model; it is the second to last step in the model. The overall objective with respect to this step in the process is to allocate the transaction price to each performance obligation in an amount that depicts the amount of consideration to which an entity expects to be entitled in exchange for transferring the promised goods or services to the customer.

2. a. *Correct.* **Previous GAAP included more than 100 revenue recognition concepts and numerous requirements for particular industries or transactions. The new guidance utilizes a contract-based approach.**

b. *Incorrect.* Ensuring strong evaluation of information systems needed to adopt the standard is not the core principle. Instead, this is a preparation step when implementing the new revenue recognition standard.

c. *Incorrect.* This is a preparation step when implementing the new revenue recognition standard. Another preparation step is to analyze and implement changes in sales or pricing strategies.

d. *Incorrect.* This is not the core principle of the new revenue recognition standard. One of the requirements for revenue recognition is that it is probable that the entity will collect the consideration to which it will be entitled.

3. a. *Incorrect.* The new guidance involves a five-step model. It includes identifying the contract with the customer, identifying performance obligations, determining transaction price, allocating transaction price to performance obligations, and finally recognizing revenue when each performance obligation is satisfied.

b. *Correct.* **The guidance requires a cohesive set of disclosure requirements intended to provide users of financial statements with information about an organization's contracts with customers.**

c. *Incorrect.* The new guidance utilizes a contract-based approach for recognizing revenue. As a result, it increases comparability across industries and capital markets.

d. *Incorrect.* This is not an impact of the new guidance. Instead, it includes a single model (not dual model) to consider variable consideration including rebates, discounts, bonuses, right of return, etc.

4. a. *Correct.* **Equitability is not one of the common-law elements of a contract. Instead, the common-law elements of a contract include agreement, consideration, and capacity.**

b. *Incorrect.* Agreement is one of the common-law elements of a contract. The agreement can be either written, verbal, or implied.

c. *Incorrect.* Consideration is one of the common-law elements of a contract. This can include anything of value including from a future action.

d. *Incorrect.* Capacity is one of the common-law elements of a contract. This relates to the fact that the person (or entity) has the ability to enter into a binding contract. To have capacity, a person must be of sound mind and have reached the age of majority.

5. a. *Incorrect.* Resources consumed is an example of an input method, not an output method. Another example of an input method is time elapsed.

b. *Incorrect.* Labor hours expended is an example of an input method, not an output method. Another example of an input method is costs incurred.

c. *Incorrect.* Machine hours used is an example of an input method. If a performance obligation is not satisfied over time, the obligation and revenue recognized should be considered satisfied at a point in time when control is transferred.

d. *Correct.* **Units produced is a type of output method. Additional examples of output methods include, but are not limited to, time elapsed and units delivered.**

6. a. *Incorrect.* To apply the standard, original equipment manufacturers (OEMs) must look at the manner in which they evaluate incentives. Furthermore, automotive parts suppliers (APSs) must change the way they evaluate long-term supply contracts.

b. *Incorrect.* Under the new standard, the percentage-of-completion method must be used instead of the completed contracts method when certain criteria are met.

c. *Correct.* **Before revenue can be recognized, there must be a valid contract with a customer, the software must exist and be delivered, the price must be independent of the quantity of users, and there must be no concessions that make the price uncollectible.**

d. *Incorrect.* For the biotech industry, complex arrangements with multiple promised goods/services (e.g., a medical device combined with installation services and a maintenance agreement) will require careful consideration to determine whether they have separate performance obligations.

¶ 10,103 MODULE 2—CHAPTER 3

1. a. *Incorrect.* The Accounting and Review Services Committee is the AICPA's senior committee for compilations or reviews and is designated to issue pronouncements in connection with the unaudited financial statements or other unaudited financial information of nonpublic entities.

b. *Incorrect.* The focus of the Assurance Services Executive Committee is to continuously anticipate, identify, assess, and address significant developments and opportunities relating to emerging assurance and advisory needs.

c. *Correct.* **The ASB is responsible for auditing, attestation, and quality control applicable to the performance and issuance of audit and attestation reports for non-issuers and the promulgation of Statements on Auditing Standards.**

d. *Incorrect.* The Center for Audit Quality is a public policy organization fostering high-quality performance by public company auditors and advocating policies and standards that promote public company auditors' objectivity, effectiveness, and responsiveness to dynamic market conditions.

2. a. *Incorrect.* Reportable events are events or transactions that occur subsequent to the balance-sheet date but prior to the issuance of the financial statements, which have a material effect on the financial statements and therefore require adjustment or disclosure in the statements.

b. *Incorrect.* KAMs are matters that were communicated with those charged with governance and, in the auditor's professional judgment, were of most significance in the audit of the financial statements of the current period.

c. *Correct.* **A CAM is a matter arising from the audit of the financial statements that was communicated or required to be communicated to the audit committee that relates to accounts or disclosures that are material to the financial statements and involved especially challenging, subjective, or complex auditor judgment.**

d. *Incorrect.* A control deficiency is a deficiency in the design or operation of a control that does not allow management or employees, in the normal course of performing their assigned functions, to prevent or detect misstatements on a timely basis.

3. a. *Incorrect.* This section addresses the auditor's responsibilities in an audit of financial statements with respect to evaluating whether there is substantial doubt about the entity's ability to continue as a going concern.

b. *Correct.* **This section addresses the auditor's responsibility to form an opinion on the financial statements. It also addresses the form and content of the auditor's report issued as a result of an audit of financial statements.**

c. *Incorrect.* This section addresses the user auditor's responsibility for obtaining sufficient appropriate audit evidence in an audit of the financial statements of a user entity that uses one or more service organizations.

d. *Incorrect.* This section addresses the independent auditor's overall responsibilities when conducting an audit of financial statements in accordance with GAAS.

4. a. *Incorrect.* A qualified opinion states that, except for the effects of the matter(s) to which the qualification relates, the financial statements present fairly, in all material respects, the financial position, results of operations, and cash flows of the entity in conformity with GAAP.

b. *Correct.* **A modified opinion is issued when the auditor concludes that a modification to the auditor's opinion on the financial statements is necessary. The form and content of the auditor's report is affected when the auditor expresses a modified opinion.**

c. *Incorrect.* An adverse opinion states that the financial statements do not present fairly the financial position, results of operations, or cash flows of the entity in conformity with GAAP.

d. *Incorrect.* A disclaimer of opinion states that the auditor does not express an opinion on the financial statements.

5. a. *Correct.* **This section addresses the auditor's responsibilities in agreeing upon the terms of the audit engagement with management and, when appropriate, those charged with governance.**

b. *Incorrect.* This section addresses the auditor's responsibility to prepare audit documentation for an audit of financial statements.

c. *Incorrect.* This section addresses the auditor's responsibility to consider laws and regulations in an audit of financial statements.

d. *Incorrect.* This section addresses the auditor's responsibility to communicate with those charged with governance in an audit of financial statements.

6. a. *Incorrect.* The PCAOB oversees the audits of public companies in order to protect the interests of investors and further the public interest in the preparation of audit reports.

b. *Correct.* **The FASB is the standard-setting body responsible for establishing and improving generally accepted accounting principles (GAAP).**

c. *Incorrect.* The AICPA is a professional organization responsible for setting ethical standards for the profession and U.S. auditing standards.

d. *Incorrect.* The GAO is part of the legislative branch of the government that provides auditing, evaluation, and investigative services for the U.S. Congress.

¶ 10,104 MODULE 2—CHAPTER 4

1. a. *Incorrect.* This SAS addresses the auditor's responsibilities in the audit of financial statements relating to the entity's ability to continue as a going concern and the implications for the auditor's report.

b. *Incorrect.* This SAS address the auditor's responsibility to form an opinion on the financial statements. It also addresses the form and content of the auditor's report issued as a result of an audit of financial statements.

c. *Incorrect.* This SAS addresses the auditor's responsibilities relating to other information, whether financial or nonfinancial information (other than financial statements and the auditor's report thereon), included in an entity's annual report.

d. *Correct.* **SAS No. 138 amends various AU-Cs in AICPA Professional Standards, to align the materiality concepts discussed in AICPA Professional Standards with the description of materiality used by the U.S. judicial system.**

2. a. *Incorrect.* **Note that the materiality concept applies in a wide variety of contexts, such as accounting, reporting, business, financial, legal, risk and, more recently, environmental, social, and governance nonfinancial issues.**

b. *Correct.* This is the correct effective date for SAS No. 138. The history of the concept of materiality dates back to 1867, when the English Court introduced the term *material* by referring to "relevant, not negligible fact" that emerged in the judgment of the false accounting case concerning the Central Railways of Venezuela.

c. *Incorrect.* This is the incorrect effective date for SAS No. 138. Regarding materiality, it has quickly become essential for stakeholder engagement exercises and topic mapping while appearing as a keyword in consultant pitches.

d. *Incorrect.* This is the incorrect effective date for SAS No. 138. Instead, it is effective at an earlier date. Note that the ASB believes that, because the revised definition is aligned with the FASB, the revised description is substantially consistent with current U.S. firm practices with respect to determining and applying materiality in an audit or attest engagement, and accordingly U.S. practice is neither expected nor intended to change.

3. a. *Incorrect.* In the context of the sustainability or nonfinancial reporting, one of the statements of the common principles of materiality by the Corporate Reporting Dialogue (CRD) indicates that "material information is that which is reasonably capable of making a difference to the proper evaluation of the issue at hand."

b. *Incorrect.* The U.S. Supreme Court says information is material if there is "a substantial likelihood that the disclosure of the omitted fact would have been viewed by the reasonable investor as having significantly altered the 'total mix' of information made available."

c. *Correct.* From a regulatory perspective, there are a number of definitions of materiality or material information. The SEC's stance is that it will not prescribe issue specific disclosures (i.e., companies are in charge of assessing material risks).

d. *Incorrect.* The International Financial Reporting Standards (IFRS) Foundation defines materiality as the following: "Information is material if omitting, misstating or obscuring it could reasonably be expected to influence the decisions that the primary users of general purpose financial statements make on the basis of those financial statements, which provide financial information about a specific reporting entity."

4. a. *Incorrect.* SSARS No. 21 relates to the general principles for engagements performed in accordance with statements on standards for accounting and review services.

b. *Incorrect.* This standard contains amendments to revise applicability of SSARSs and to clarify and revise requirements throughout AR-C Sections 60, 70, 80, and 90.

c. *Incorrect.* This standard addresses situations in which an accountant is engaged to perform a compilation or review of financial statements in accordance with SSARSs when either (a) the financial statements have been prepared in accordance with a financial reporting framework generally accepted in another country not adopted by a body designated by the Council of the AICPA, or (b) the compilation or review engagement is to be performed in accordance with both SSARSs and another set of compilation or review standards.

d. *Correct.* SSARS No. 25 amends SSARS No. 21, *Statements on Standards for Accounting and Review Services: Clarification and Recodification*. It includes amendments to Sections 60, 70, 80, and 90.

5. a. *Incorrect.* This is a basis of accounting that the entity uses to record cash receipts and disbursements and modifications of the cash basis having substantial support (e.g., recording depreciation on fixed assets).

b. *Correct.* Regulatory basis is a basis of accounting that the entity uses to comply with the requirements or financial reporting provisions of a regulatory agency to whose jurisdiction the entity is subject (e.g., a basis of accounting that

insurance companies use pursuant to the accounting practices prescribed or permitted by a state insurance department).

c. Incorrect. This is a basis of accounting that the entity uses to file its tax return for the period covered by the financial statements.

d. Incorrect. This is a basis of accounting that the entity uses to comply with an agreement between the entity and one or more third parties other than the accountant.

6. a. Incorrect. Section 60 relates to "General Principles for Engagements Performed in Accordance with Statements on Standards for Accounting and Review Services." It does not specifically relate to reviews of financial statements.

b. Incorrect. Section 70 relates to the preparation of financial statements. Although it was amended by SSARS No. 25, it does not relate to reviews of financial statements.

c. Incorrect. Section 80 relates to compilation engagements. Although it was amended by SSARS No. 25, it does not relate specifically to reviews of financial statements.

d. Correct. Section 90 relates specifically to review engagements. In a review of financial statements, the accountant expresses a conclusion regarding the entity's financial statements in accordance with an applicable financial reporting framework.

¶ 10,105 MODULE 2—CHAPTER 5

1. a. Correct. The purpose of Regulation S-K is to lay out reporting requirements for various SEC filings used by public companies.

b. Incorrect. Regulation S-K does not lay out the specific form and content of financial statements; rather, Regulation S-X does.

c. Incorrect. Regulation S-K is broader than just laying out reporting requirements for the Form 10-K.

d. Incorrect. Regulation S-K does relate to the form and content (that is Regulation S-X). In addition, the guidance is not applicable for non-public companies.

2. a. Incorrect. The purpose of the executive overview not to provide "detailed" information about the organization's operations.

b. Correct. The purpose is to provide a big-picture outlook of the company's operations.

c. Incorrect. The purpose is not to provide detailed information about how the organization finances its operations. This is done in other sections of MD&A along with the financial statements.

d. Incorrect. The purpose is not to provide detailed information about critical estimates. This is done in the MD&A section on critical estimates.

3. a. Incorrect. Off-balance sheet transactions do not appear on the income statement.

b. Incorrect. Off-balance sheet transactions do not appear on the cash flow statement.

c. Incorrect. Off-balance sheet transactions are not defined as those that are not part of the parent company.

d. Correct. Off-balance sheet transactions are transactions or agreements that are not required to be reported on the balance sheet.

4. a. *Incorrect.* The update to Item 303 did not eliminate the requirement to discuss off-balance sheet arrangements.

b. *Correct.* **The update to Item 303 eliminated the requirement to discuss the impact of inflation.**

c. *Incorrect.* The update to Item 303 did not eliminate the requirement to disclose capital resource issues.

d. *Incorrect.* The update to Item 303 did not eliminate the requirement to discuss critical accounting estimates.

5. a. *Correct.* **The disclosure was revised to include changes that are reasonably likely to cause a material change in the relationship between costs and revenues.**

b. *Incorrect.* The disclosure did not address discussion of changes to assets and liabilities.

c. *Incorrect.* The disclosure did not address discussions that have a significant impact on equity.

d. *Incorrect.* The discussion did specifically indicate the changes were related to those that had a quantifiable significant change in the relationship between costs and revenues.

6. a. *Incorrect.* The requirement does not include providing a definition of where the metric came from.

b. *Correct.* **The requirement includes providing a statement indicating the reasons why the metric provides useful information to investors.**

c. *Incorrect.* The requirement does not include a statement explaining what reliance the external auditors put on the metric.

d. *Incorrect.* The requirement does not include a statement explaining what reliance investors should place on the metric.

¶ 10,106 MODULE 2—CHAPTER 6

1. a. *Incorrect.* We are increasing our reliance on technology in business and increasing our use of electronic data storage.

b. *Incorrect.* Our access to data is increasing, as is our use of electronic communications.

c. *Correct.* **During a public company audit, auditors are looking for disclosure of nonpublic company information. Employees can easily share this type of information through social media. There are potential insider trading risks associated with social media.**

d. *Incorrect.* Bitcoin is only one small aspect of what Blockchain can do. Blockchain was designed to verify things such as documents, dates that transactions were signed, when transactions were posted, and that shipments were shipped. Auditors may need to audit the Blockchain.

2. a. *Incorrect.* Data velocity is the speed at which data is generated, collected, and processed.

b. *Correct.* **Data volume is the amount of data being processed**

c. *Incorrect.* Data variety indicates the different types of data that are available.

d. *Incorrect.* Data veracity indicates how good or valid the data is.

3. a. *Correct.* **An appropriate method for statistical sampling is random sampling. With random sampling, all items have an equal chance of selection.**

b. *Incorrect.* In systematic sampling, every *n* th item is selected with a random start within the *n* interval.

c. *Incorrect.* Haphazard selection involves selecting sample items without intentional bias.

d. *Incorrect.* When using block selection, a group of contiguous transactions, such as invoices in a sequence, are audited.

4. a. *Incorrect.* Prescriptive analytics allows the users to choose the best options. This is not used very often in external auditing.

b. *Incorrect.* When using predictive analytics, auditors are looking for trends to predict what should happen in the future.

c. *Incorrect.* When using diagnostic analytics, auditors are looking for causes of errors.

d. *Correct.* **Descriptive analytics looks at past performance. In an audit, auditors are typically looking at what happened in the last period.**

5. a. *Incorrect.* Confirmation bias involves not looking at evidence that could suggest the person is wrong.

b. *Incorrect.* Bounded awareness involves not confirming accounts because they look right to the auditor.

c. *Correct.* **Affinity bias involves trusting others who are like you. For example, a CPA will trust other CPAs.**

d. *Incorrect.* Priming is the act of being influenced by other people or data.

6. a. *Correct.* **Although you might expect each digit to occur about 11.1 percent of the time, a leading digit of 1 occurs about 30.1 percent of the time.**

b. *Incorrect.* A leading digit of 3 occurs about 12.5 percent of the time. There are two other digits that have a higher percentage chance of occurring.

c. *Incorrect.* While 9 is the highest leading possible digit, it occurs as the leading digit the lowest percentage as compared to the other digits, coming in at 4.6 percent.

d. *Incorrect.* You would expect each digit to occur approximately 11.1 percent of the time, but that is not the case.

¶ 10,107 MODULE 3—CHAPTER 7

1. a. *Incorrect.* Gabriel Tarde developed the theory of differential reinforcement.

b. *Correct.* **Ronald Akers developed the social learning theory, which is combined elements of the differential reinforcement and differential association theories.**

c. *Incorrect.* Edwin Sutherland developed the theory of differential association.

d. *Incorrect.* Donald Cressey developed the fraud triangle.

2. a. *Incorrect.* Duplicate invoice fraud involves sending multiple invoices hoping to get paid more than once.

b. *Incorrect.* Receivables dumping occurs when employees assign collectible accounts to a collection for a kickback or other compensation.

c. *Correct.* **Re-aging occurs when new accounts receivable are created to pay off aged receivables to make the receivables look current.**

d. *Incorrect.* Skimming involves taking payments before they are recorded in the accounting system.

3. a. *Incorrect.* Cash larceny is stealing cash that has been recorded in the accounting system from a register, deposit, or safe.

b. *Incorrect.* Kiting is done with checks, not with cash.

c. *Correct.* **Skimming is a fraud where employees or volunteers steal cash or checks before transactions are entered into the accounting system.**

d. *Incorrect.* Cash drawer loans involve employees putting personal NSF checks in their cash drawer in exchange for cash.

4. a. *Incorrect.* Expensing items and then selling them on the Internet is a way employees commit expense reimbursement fraud.

b. *Incorrect.* Purchasing and canceling extended warranties is a way employees commit expense reimbursement fraud.

c. *Correct.* **Entertaining customers is not considered fraud.**

d. *Incorrect.* Employees commit expense reimbursement fraud through shell companies.

5. a. *Incorrect.* The security thread in a $5 bill glows blue under a black light.

b. *Correct.* **The security thread in a $20 bill is green when viewed with a black light.**

c. *Incorrect.* A black light will show a yellow security thread in a $50 bill.

d. *Incorrect.* Pink is the color of the security thread in a $100 bill.

6. a. *Incorrect.* A bill and hold scheme is a revenue scheme.

b. *Incorrect.* Lapping is an accounts receivable fraud.

c. *Incorrect.* Cooking the books is financial statement fraud.

d. *Correct.* **Short shipping is one of the many types of inventory fraud.**

7. a. *Incorrect.* Phishing uses email to obtain personal information or to get you to download malware by clicking on a link.

b. *Correct.* **Ransomware is a type of malware that is placed on a computer and then encrypts all of the files on the computer.**

c. *Incorrect.* Spoofing hides the true origin of an email or website to make it look legitimate.

d. *Incorrect.* Spyware tracks your information; it does not encrypt it.

8. a. *Incorrect.* This is an example of skimming, not a data breach.

b. *Incorrect.* This is an example of shoulder surfing, which is not a data breach.

c. *Correct.* **Stealing information from a computer is an example of a data breach. Organizations are increasingly susceptible to this type of fraud.**

d. *Incorrect.* This is an example of criminal identity theft, not a data breach.

¶10,107

9. a. *Incorrect.* Cash drawer loans involve postdated checks from an employee's bank account.

b. *Incorrect.* Skimming is taking funds before they are entered into the cash register or accounting system.

c. *Correct.* **In criminal identity theft, fraudsters use a victim's identity to open businesses and bank accounts and then process stolen checks and credit cards through these accounts.**

d. *Incorrect.* Refund frauds are committed by entering false returns into the cash register.

10. a. *Incorrect.* During a typical business identity theft scheme, the fraudsters use the business name to obtain loans or credit.

b. *Incorrect.* During a typical financial identity theft scheme, the fraudsters use the personal information to obtain financial benefits.

c. *Correct.* **Fraudulent use of someone's professional license is considered professional identity theft. Because professional licenses are a matter of public record, it is relatively easy to commit this type of fraud.**

d. *Incorrect.* During a typical employment fraud scheme, the fraudster uses the name and Social Security number of the victim to obtain employment.

11. a. *Incorrect.* A data breach involves obtaining confidential information from a computer system.

b. *Correct.* **In this type of fraud, fraudsters input stolen IDs and passwords into software that searches the Internet for websites where the stolen IDs and passwords work and then notifies a human operator that access has been gained so they can determine if there is any value in the website that was illegally accessed.**

c. *Incorrect.* Ransomware encrypts data on a system.

d. *Incorrect.* Phishing is done with email.

12. a. *Correct.* **The three steps of money laundering are placement, layering, and integration.**

b. *Incorrect.* Opportunity is part of the fraud triangle, not one of the three steps of money laundering.

c. *Incorrect.* Conversion is an element of fraud, not one of the three steps of money laundering.

d. *Incorrect.* Rationalization is part of the fraud triangle, not one of the three steps of money laundering.

Index

References are to paragraph (¶) numbers.

¶ 10,200 Glossary

Asset misappropriation: The theft of either tangible or intangible assets.

Audit risk model: A model which states that the audit risk is equal to the inherent risk times the control risk times the detection risk, or AR = IR × CR × DR.

Auditing Standards Board (ASB): The senior technical committee designated by the American Institute of Certified Public Accountants (AICPA) to issue auditing, attestation, and quality control statements, standards, and guidance to certified public accountants for non-public company audits.

Available-for-sale securities: Investments not classified as either trading securities or as held-to-maturity securities.

Benford's Law: A theory regarding the distribution of the first digits of large sets of data.

Bitcoin: A type of virtual currency.

Bribery: Illicit payments for information or actions paid to corrupt employees or officials.

Comparative financial statements: A complete set of financial statements for one or more prior periods included for comparison with the financial statements of the current period.

Comparative information: Prior period information presented for purposes of comparison with current period amounts or disclosures that is not in the form of a complete set of financial statements. Comparative information includes prior period information presented as condensed financial statements or summarized financial information.

Condensed financial statements: Historical financial information that is presented in less detail than a complete set of financial statements, in accordance with an appropriate financial reporting framework. Condensed financial statements may be separately presented as unaudited financial information or may be presented as comparative information.

Conflict of interest: Occurs when an employee, manager, or executive has an undisclosed economic or personal interest in a transaction that adversely affects that person's employer.

Conscious bias: Prejudice, of which one is aware, in favor of or against one thing, person, or group compared with another.

Contract: An agreement between two or more parties that creates enforceable rights and obligations.

Control risk: The risk of a material misstatement in the financial statements arising due to absence or failure in the operation of relevant controls of the entity.

COVID-19: Stands for *coronavirus disease 2019*. A mild to severe respiratory illness caused by a coronavirus named *SARS-COV-2*. COVID-19 spread at a rapid pace in early 2020, resulting in a pandemic.

Critical audit matter (CAM): Any matter arising from the audit of the financial statements that was communicated or was required to be communicated to the audit committee, and that relates to accounts or disclosures that are material to the financial statements and involved especially challenging, subjective, or complex auditor judgment.

Data analytics: The science of analyzing raw data in order to make conclusions about that information.

Data breach: The release or taking of data from a secure source to an unsecured third-party location (computer).

Data mining: A process that uses mathematical algorithms to detect hidden patterns in data.

Denial of service attack: Cyberattack that occurs when criminals use their own computer networks or botnets to bring down a website or computer system by overloading its capabilities, thereby crashing the system.

Direct financing lease: From the perspective of a lessor, a lease that meets none of the criteria as a sales-type lease but meets other specific criteria.

Discount rate: For a lessee, the discount rate for the lease is the rate implicit in the lease unless that rate cannot be readily determined. In that case, the lessee is required to use its incremental borrowing rate. For a lessor, the discount rate for the lease is the rate implicit in the lease.

Effective interest rate: The rate of return implicit in the loan, that is, the contractual interest rate adjusted for any net deferred loan fees or costs, premium, or discount existing at the origination or acquisition of the loan.

Factoring fraud: A type of fraud that occurs when management inflates the value of accounts receivable in order to qualify for a loan using the receivables as collateral.

Finance lease: From the perspective of a lessee, a lease that meets one or more of the criteria in Accounting Standards Codification (ASC) paragraph 842-10-25-2.

Financial asset: Cash, evidence of an ownership interest in an entity, or a contract that conveys to one entity a right to either receive cash or another financial instrument from a second entity, or to exchange other financial instruments on potentially favorable terms with the second entity.

Financial statement fraud: Fraud designed to "cook the books" and present false information on the financial statements.

Fraud: A deception deliberately practiced in order to secure unfair or unlawful gain.

Fraud triangle: The theory developed by Dr. Donald Cressey explaining why individuals commit occupational fraud. The three components of the fraud triangle are pressure, rationalization, and opportunity.

General purpose financial statements: Financial statements prepared in accordance with a general-purpose framework.

General purpose framework: A financial reporting framework designed to meet the common financial information needs of a wide range of users.

Ghost employee: A phantom employee that exists only on the books.

Hacker: Someone attempting to gain access to a computer for malicious or illegal purposes.

Identity theft: Broadly defined as the use of one person's identity or personally identifying information by another person without his or her permission. Identity theft is a type of fraud and can be committed against an individual or organization.

Initial direct costs: Incremental costs of a lease that would not have been incurred if the lease had not been obtained.

Input method: Revenue recognition based on the entity's effort to satisfy a performance obligation relative to the total expected effort.

Inquiry: Consists of seeking information of knowledgeable persons within or outside the entity.

Key performance indicator (KPI): A measure used to evaluate how effectively an organization is meeting its performance objectives.

Kickback: The giving or receiving anything of value to influence a business decision.

Lapping: A fraud scheme that involves stealing payments from one customer and covering the theft with payments stolen from other customers.

Larceny: Theft.

Lease modification: A change to the terms and conditions of a contract that results in a change in the scope of or the consideration for a lease (e.g., a change to the terms and conditions of the contract that adds or terminates the right to use one or more underlying assets or extends or shortens the contractual lease term).

Lease: A contract, or part of a contract, that conveys the right to control the use of identified property, plant, or equipment (an identified asset) for a period of time in exchange for consideration.

Lease term: The noncancellable period for which a lessee has the right to use an underlying asset plus periods covered by an option to extend the lease if the lessee is reasonably certain to exercise that option, periods covered by an option to terminate the lease if the lessee is reasonably certain not to exercise that option, and periods covered by an option to extend (or not to terminate) the lease in which exercise of the option is controlled by the lessor.

Limited assurance: A level of assurance that is less than the reasonable assurance obtained in an audit engagement but is at an acceptable level as the basis for the conclusion expressed in the accountant's review report.

Malware: Software that is placed on computers or cell phones to hijack the computers, steal data, or encrypt the data for ransom.

Management's Discussion and Analysis (MD&A): The portion of a public company's annual report (or quarterly filing) in which management addresses the company's performance. It is intended to be a narrative explanation of the financial statements and statistical data the registrant believes will enhance a reader's understanding of its financial condition along with results of operations.

Misappropriation: Obtaining something of value, or avoiding an obligation by deception or false statements; a type of fraud.

Modified conclusion: A qualified conclusion or an adverse conclusion.

Money laundering: Taking funds from an illegal source, hiding the source of funds, and making the funds available for use without legal restrictions or penalties.

Occupational fraud: Fraud occurring in the workplace or relating to employment.

Off-balance sheet arrangements: Transactions or agreements that are not required to be reported on the balance sheet. These arrangements can impact revenues, expenses, and cash flows. Off-balance sheet items are in contrast to loans, debt, and equity, which do appear on the balance sheet.

Operating lease: From the perspective of a lessee, any lease other than a finance lease. From the perspective of a lessor, any lease other than a sales-type lease or a direct financing lease.

Output method: Revenue recognition based on the value transferred to the customer relative to the remaining value to be transferred.

Performance obligation: A promise in a contract with a customer to transfer to the customer either a good or service (or a bundle of goods or services) that is distinct or a series of distinct goods or services that are substantially the same and that have the same pattern of transfer to the customer.

Pervasive: A term used, in the context of misstatements, to describe the effects on the financial statements of misstatements.

Pharming: A fraud scheme in which a virus or malicious software is secretly loaded onto the victim's computer and hijacks the web browser.

Phishing: A technique used by fraudsters to obtain personal information for purposes of identity theft. This theft can include sending illegitimate emails asking for personal information.

Professional skepticism: An attitude that includes a questioning mind, being alert to conditions that may indicate possible misstatement due to fraud or error, and a critical assessment of review evidence.

Purchased financial assets with credit deterioration: Acquired individual financial assets (or acquired groups of financial assets with similar risk characteristics) that as of the date of acquisition have experienced a more-than-insignificant deterioration in credit quality since origination, as determined by an acquirer's assessment.

Registrant: An issuer making an initial filing, including amendments, under the Securities Act of 1933 or the Securities Exchange Act of 1934; or a registrant that files periodic reports under the Investment Company Act.

Regulation S-K: A prescribed regulation under the U.S. Securities Act of 1933 that lays out reporting requirements for various Securities and Exchange Commission (SEC) filings used by public companies.

Regulation S-X: A prescribed regulation in the United States that lays out the specific form and content of financial reports, specifically the financial statements of public companies.

Review evidence: Information used by the accountant to provide a reasonable basis for obtaining limited assurance.

Right-of-use asset: An asset that represents a lessee's right to use an underlying asset for the lease term.

Sales-type lease: From the perspective of a lessor, a lease that meets one or more of the criteria in Accounting Standards Codification (ASC) paragraph 842-10-25-2.

Sampling: The application of an audit procedure to less than 100 percent of the items within an account balance or class of transactions for the purpose of evaluating some characteristic of the balance or class.

Shell companies: Legal business entities created for the purpose of committing fraud. There is no actual business, but only paperwork.

Skimming: Removal of cash from a victim entity prior to its entry in an accounting system.

Smishing: A fraud scheme similar to phishing and vishing, but it is done using text messages rather than phone calls or email.

Spoofing: Term used to describe fraudulent e-mail activity in which the sender's address or other parts of the e-mail header are altered to appear as though the e-mail originated from a different source.

Stand-alone selling price: The price at which an entity would sell a promised good or service separately to a customer.

Transaction price: The amount of consideration to which an entity expects to be entitled in exchange for transferring promised goods or services to a customer, excluding amounts collected on behalf of third parties.

Trojan horse: A malware program that is disguised as something else. Users assume it is a beneficial program when it fact it is not. Trojans horses are often used to insert spyware onto computers.

Unconscious bias: The attitudes or stereotypes that affect one's understanding, actions, and decisions in an unconscious manner. Also known as *implicit bias*.

Unmodified opinion: The opinion expressed by the auditor when the auditor concludes that the financial statements are presented fairly, in all material respects, in accordance with the applicable financial reporting framework.

Vishing: A fraud scheme similar to phishing, but it occurs over the phone rather than over the Internet.

¶ 10,300 Final Exam Instructions

To complete your Final Exam go to **cchcpelink.com/printcpe**, click on the title of the exam you wish to complete and add it to your shopping cart (you will need to register with CCH CPELink if you have not already). Click **Proceed to Checkout** and enter your credit card information. Click **Place Order** to complete your purchase of the final exam. The final exam will be available in **My Dashboard** under **My Account**.

This Final Exam is divided into three Modules. There is a grading fee for each Final Exam submission.

Online Processing Fee:	Recommended CPE:
$90.00 for Module 1	4 hours for Module 1
$154.00 for Module 2	7 hours for Module 2
$90.00 for Module 3	4 hours for Module 3
$334.00 for all Modules	15 hours for all Modules

Instructions for purchasing your CPE Tests and accessing them after purchase are provided on the **cchcpelink.com/printcpe** website. **Please note, manual grading is no longer available for Top Accounting and Auditing Issues. All answer sheets must be submitted online for grading and processing.**

Recommended CPE credit is based on a 50-minute hour. Because CPE requirements vary from state to state and among different licensing agencies, please contact your CPE governing body for information on your CPE requirements and the applicability of a particular course for your requirements

Expiration Date: December 31, 2021

Evaluation: To help us provide you with the best possible products, please take a moment to fill out the course Evaluation located after your Final Exam.

Wolters Kluwer, CCH is registered with the National Association of State Boards of Accountancy (NASBA) as a sponsor of continuing professional education on the National Registry of CPE Sponsors. State boards of accountancy have final authority on the acceptance of individual courses for CPE credit. Complaints regarding registered sponsors may be submitted to the National Registry of CPE Sponsors through its website: www.learningmarket.org.

Additional copies of this course may be downloaded from **cchcpelink.com/printcpe**. Printed copies of the course are available for $4.50 by calling 1-800-344-3734 (ask for product 10024493-0008).

¶ 10,301 FINAL EXAM QUESTIONS: MODULE 1

1. Which ASC topic provides the guidance for the new lease accounting standard?

    a. ASC Topic 840

    b. ASC Topic 842

    c. ASC Topic 845

    d. ASC Topic 918

2. Which of the following identifies the new name for a capital lease?

    a. Finance lease

    b. Leveraged lease

    c. Synthetic lease

    d. Structured lease

3. Which type of lease modification requires a lessee to account for the modification as a separate contract?

    a. The lessee either fully or partially terminates an existing lease.

    b. The modification grants the lessee additional right-of-use with a commensurate increase in the lease payments.

    c. The lessee extends the term of the lease through the exercise of a contractual option.

    d. The lessor grants the lessee additional right-of-use prescribed by the original contract.

4. Lessees and lessors are required to adopt the new lease standard and recognize and measure leases at the beginning of the earliest period presented using which approach?

    a. Prospective

    b. Modified prospective

    c. Retroactive

    d. Modified retrospective

5. The FASB allows a private company to elect to use which rate so long as the company applies this methodology to all leases and discloses that it has elected to use the practical expedient?

    a. Incremental borrowing rate

    b. Weighted average cost of capital

    c. Risk-free rate

    d. 10-year Treasury rate

6. If a lease modification is not accounted for as a separate contract, then a company _____ reassess the classification of the lease as of the effective date of the modification based on the modified terms and conditions.

    a. Is required to

    b. May be required to

    c. Is not required to

    d. Would likely

7. The new credit losses standard will replace the current _____ approach with a (n) _____ model for instruments measured at amortized cost and requires entities to record allowances for available-for-sale debt securities rather than reduce the carrying amount.

    a. Incurred loss, worst case

    b. Expected loss, incurred loss

    c. Incurred loss, expected loss

    d. Expected loss, worst case

8. The new credit losses standard must be adopted using which type of transition approach?

    a. Modified retrospective

    b. Retrospective

    c. Modified prospective

    d. Prospective

9. Which of the following identifies the new effective date of the credit losses standard for calendar-year public business entities that are not SEC filers?

    a. 2021

    b. 2022

    c. 2023

    d. 2024

10. The SEC normally would expect companies to maintain written supporting documentation for each of the following decisions and processes related to the new credit losses standard, *except:*

    a. Summary or consolidation of the allowance for credit losses balance

    b. Validation of the allowance for credit losses methodology

    c. Periodic adjustments to the allowance for credit losses

    d. Differences in methodology applied as compared to ASC 310 requirements

11. The new revenue recognition standard is effective for public companies for annual reporting periods beginning after what date?

    a. December 15, 2016

    b. December 15, 2017

    c. December 15, 2018

    d. December 15, 2019

12. Of the following industries, which one is expected to experience the least amount of change from the new revenue recognition standard?

    a. Retail

    b. Telecommunications

    c. Construction

    d. Software

13. Once a contract with a customer has been identified, the next step in the revenue recognition model is to:

    a. Determine the transaction price.

    b. Recognize revenue as each performance obligation is satisfied.

    c. Identify performance obligations.

    d. Identify variable consideration.

14. Based on the new revenue recognition guidance, the transaction price will be allocated to each performance obligation on basis of the:

    a. Stand-alone selling price

    b. Fair market value

    c. Variable consideration

    d. Fully burdened replacement cost

15. Which of the following statements is correct if a contract is not legally enforceable or lacks commercial substance?

    a. The transaction price should be discounted.

    b. Revenue can only be recognized if the contract is material to the entity.

    c. Performance obligation should be identified.

    d. Revenue recognition must be delayed.

16. Which of the following identifies an acceptable method for measuring progress?

    a. Cost method

    b. Output method

    c. Value method

    d. Contract method

17. Consideration is classified as _____ any time it is contingent upon the occurrence or nonoccurrence of a future event.

    a. Variable

    b. Fixed

    c. Indeterminate

    d. Unknown

18. When allocating the transaction price to performance obligations, which of the following estimation methods uses the price a customer would pay for the good or service in market?

    a. Expected cost plus margin

    b. Residual

    c. Adjusted market assessment

    d. Net realizable value

19. To apply the updated revenue recognition standard, parts suppliers for the _____ industry must change the way they evaluate long-term supply contracts.

    a. Automotive

    b. Biotech

    c. Software

    d. Electronics

20. Under the new revenue recognition standard, which of the following methods will likely be used only in rare circumstances?

    a. Percentage-of-completion method

    b. Input method

    c. Completed contracts method

    d. Output method

¶ 10,302 FINAL EXAM QUESTIONS: MODULE 2

1. The Auditing Standards Board's strategy is to converge its standards with which organization?

  a. International Financial Reporting Standards (IFRS)

  b. International Auditing and Assurance Standards Board (IAASB)

  c. Financial Accounting Standards Board (FASB)

  d. International Accounting Standards Committee Foundation (IASCF)

2. The final PCAOB auditing standards and amendments were approved by the SEC on:

  a. October 23, 2016

  b. October 23, 2017

  c. October 23, 2018

  d. October 23, 2019

3. The updates to Statements on Auditing Standards (SAS) sections by the Accounting Standards Board (ASB) are effective on which date?

  a. December 15, 2018

  b. December 15, 2019

  c. December 15, 2020

  d. December 15, 2021

4. AU—C Section 800, *Special Considerations*, addresses audits of financial statements prepared in accordance with:

  a. Generally Accepted Auditing Standards

  b. Special purpose frameworks

  c. Reporting in a single audit

  d. International Financial Reporting Standards

5. The auditor's report should have a title that clearly indicates that it is the report of a(n):

  a. External auditor

  b. Independent third party

  c. Licensed accountant

  d. Independent auditor

6. The "Opinion" section of the auditor's report should include all the following, *except:*

  a. Identify the entity whose financial statements have been audited.

  b. State that the financial statements have been audited.

  c. Identify the title of each statement that the financial statements comprise.

  d. Refer to the internal audit report.

7. The auditors' report should name the city and state where the _____.

  a. Auditors' report is issued

  b. Company is headquartered

  c. Audit was completed

  d. Auditors home office is located

8. In performing an audit in accordance with GAAS, auditors must exercise professional _____ and maintain professional _____ throughout the audit.

    a. Appearance, judgment

    b. Judgment, independence

    c. Independence, appearance

    d. Judgment, skepticism

9. AU—C Section 570 addresses an auditor's consideration of an entity's ability to:

    a. Meet its financial obligations

    b. Maintain adequate internal controls

    c. Accurately report its financial conditions

    d. Continue as a going concern

10. SAS No. 136, *Forming an Opinion and Reporting on Financial Statements of Employee Benefit Plans Subject to ERISA*, was issued in:

    a. July 2019

    b. December 2019

    c. July 2018

    d. December 2018

11. SAS No. 138, SSAE No. 20, and SSARS No. _____ amend various AU-C, AT-C, and AR-C sections, respectively, in AICPA Professional Standards, to align the materiality concepts discussed in AICPA Professional Standards with the description of materiality used by the U.S. judicial system, and the auditing standards of the PCAOB, the SEC, and the FASB.

    a. 21

    b. 22

    c. 23

    d. 25

12. Which organization stated that it believes it is in the public interest to eliminate inconsistencies between the AICPA Professional Standards and the description of materiality used by the U.S. judicial system and other U.S. standard-setters and regulators?

    a. Auditing Standards Board (ASB)

    b. FASB Foundation

    c. International Accounting Standards Board (IASB)

    d. IFRS Foundation

13. Which organization refers to the concept of something being material if there is "a substantial likelihood that the disclosure of the omitted fact would have been viewed by the reasonable investor as having significantly altered the 'total mix' of information made available"?

    a. Corporate Reporting Dialogue

    b. U.S. Supreme Court

    c. IFRS Foundation

    d. U.S. SEC

14. Which AU-C Section was amended as a result of SAS No. 138 related to materiality in planning and performing an audit?

  a. AU-C Section 200

  b. AU-C Section 320

  c. AU-C Section 450

  d. AU-C Section 600

15. The amendments made to AU-C Section 200 (*Overall Objectives of the Independent Auditor and the Conduct of an Audit in Accordance with Generally Accepted Auditing Standards*) from SAS No. 138 are effective for audits of financial statements for periods ending on or after:

  a. December 15, 2020

  b. December 15, 2021

  c. December 15, 2022

  d. December 15, 2023

16. Which SSAE was amended as it relates to the recent changes in the concept of materiality?

  a. SSAE No. 19

  b. SSAE No. 20

  c. SSAE No. 21

  d. SSAE No. 22

17. Which section related to compilation engagements was amended as a result of SSARS No. 25?

  a. Section 60

  b. Section 70

  c. Section 80

  d. Section 90

18. Which of the following identifies a basis of accounting that the entity uses to comply with an agreement between the entity and one or more third parties other than the accountant?

  a. Contractual basis

  b. Tax basis

  c. Cash basis

  d. Regulatory basis

19. The amendments to Section 80 from SSARS No. 25 are effective for compilations of financial statements for periods ending on or after what date?

  a. December 15, 2020

  b. December 15, 2021

  c. December 15, 2022

  d. December 15, 2023

20. Which of the following is "a level of assurance that is less than the reasonable assurance obtained in an audit engagement but is at an acceptable level as the basis for the conclusion expressed in the accountant's review report"?

    a. Unreasonable assurance

    b. Moderate assurance

    c. High-level assurance

    d. Limited assurance

21. What is the purpose of Regulation S-X?

    a. To outline the requirements for reporting requirements for multiple SEC filings

    b. To provide the specific form and content of financial reports, specifically of public companies

    c. To outline the requirements for disclosing financial statement footnotes

    d. To outline the requirements around risk disclosures in the financial statements

22. Which of the following may be a section included within Management Discussion and Analysis (MD&A) of the financial statements?

    a. Trends and risks

    b. Names of the members of the board of directors

    c. Minutes of the executive meetings

    d. Compensation of executives

23. Which of the following is an example of an off-balance sheet arrangement?

    a. A contract with a new supplier

    b. A sale with a joint venture partner

    c. Derivative instruments that are classified as equity

    d. Owner's equity

24. An area updated with the MD&A disclosures is Item 301 on Selected Financial Data. What specifically did the SEC eliminate for this disclosure?

    a. References relating to contingencies and estimates

    b. References related to liabilities and legal proceedings

    c. References related to contribution to capital

    d. Reference of year-to-year comparisons

25. What was the purpose of the amendment to Item 302(a) related to Supplementary Financial Information?

    a. To eliminate the requirement to provide two years of selected quarterly financial data

    b. To eliminate the requirement to provide year to year comparisons

    c. To eliminate the requirement to provide month-to-month comparisons

    d. To eliminate the requirement to provide three months of selective data comparisons

26. Item 303(a) of MD&A outlined numerous changes to Item 303. Which of the following change(s) was (were) included?

    a. Elimination of unnecessary cross-references

    b. Addition of a requirement to discuss critical accounting estimates

    c. Elimination of the requirement to discuss the impact of inflation

    d. All of the above

27. Item 303(a)(2) deals with capital resource disclosures. What was the reason for the amendment to this area?

    a. To revise disclosure requirements to account for capital expenditures that are not necessarily capital investments

    b. To eliminate the need to account for capital expenditures that are not necessarily capital investments

    c. To minimize the disclosure requirements for capital expenditures less than $1 million

    d. To adjust the disclosure requirements for capital expenditures to eliminate the need to disclosure material cash commitments for capital expenditures

28. Item 303(a)(3)(ii) deals with the results of operations. What was the adopted change for this section?

    a. Update disclosure to require disclosure of known events that will cause a significant change in the relationship between assets and liabilities

    b. Update disclosure to require disclosure of known events that are reasonably likely to cause a material change in the relationship between costs and revenues

    c. Update disclosure to require disclosure of potential events that will cause a material change in the relationship between costs and revenues

    d. Update disclosure to require disclosure of all events considered probable of causing any change in the relationship between costs and revenues

29. Item 303(a)(5) addressed contractual obligations. What did the amendment provide for?

    a. The need for the registrant to provide a contractual obligations table

    b. The need for the registrant to provide a full narrative of all contractual obligations

    c. The need for the registrant to provide a narrative of any contractual obligation that may be subject to litigation

    d. Elimination of the need for the registrant to provide a contractual obligations table

30. The SEC made changes to requirements for key performance indicators. Which of the following is (are) items outlined as generally expected to be disclosed?

    a. A clear definition of the metric and how it is calculated

    b. A statement indicating the reasons why the metric provides useful information to investors

    c. A statement indicating how management uses the metric in managing or monitoring the performance of the business

    d. All of the above

31. Data analytics can be used in all aspects of an audit. How can data analytics be used as a test of details?

    a. Cash receipts to sales invoice matching

    b. Regression analysis

    c. Analysis of customer accounts – this could also have a test of details

    d. Analysis of preliminary general ledger account balances

32. With big data analytics, the auditor focuses on:

    a. Causation

    b. Diagnosis analytics

    c. Descriptive analytics

    d. Predictive analytics

33. Unstructured data includes:

    a. Audit trails

    b. Email

    c. Databases

    d. Transactional data

34. The basis for sampling in an audit is:

    a. Exploratory analysis

    b. Predictive analysis

    c. Inferential analysis

    d. Confirmatory analysis

35. Which risk is determined by an auditor's evaluation of the design and effectiveness of the client's internal controls?

    a. Audit risk

    b. Control risk

    c. Detection risk

    d. Inherent risk

36. The use of algorithms to identify data in large databases is:

    a. Descriptive statistics

    b. Statistical analysis

    c. Data visualization

    d. Data mining

37. An example of an auditor's conscious bias that could affect data analytics in an audit is:

    a. Affinity bias

    b. Group think

    c. Anchoring

    d. Personal relationships

38. The type of unconscious bias where an auditor allows his or her emotions to control decisions is called:

    a. Blind spot bias

    b. Ambiguity effect

    c. Empathy gap

    d. Negativity bias

39. When using Benford's Law, data sets to be examined must be:

    a. Qualitative

    b. Randomly generated

    c. Assigned numbers

    d. From small sets of data

40. Which of the following is true regarding Benford's Law?

    a. 1 occurs as the leading digit 30.1 percent of the time.

    b. 2 occurs as the leading digit 9.7 percent of the time.

    c. 9 occurs as the leading digit the highest percentage of time as compared to the other digits.

    d. Each digit occurs as the leading digit about 11 percent of the time.

¶ 10,303 FINAL EXAM QUESTIONS: MODULE 3

1. Which of the following cyber frauds is used to hide the origin of an email?
   a. Phishing
   b. Pharming
   c. Whaling
   d. Spoofing

2. What is the most common way to pay for stolen credit card numbers purchased over the Internet?
   a. Cash
   b. Bitcoin
   c. Credit card
   d. Check

3. Bid rigging normally falls under which type of corruption?
   a. Conflict of interest
   b. Bribery
   c. Illegal gratuity
   d. Economic extortion

4. Which type of corruption involves the misuse of political office?
   a. Nepotism
   b. Graft
   c. Bribery
   d. Illegal gratuity

5. Which of the following types of corruption payment is most likely to be associated with economic extortion?
   a. Gifts
   b. Hospitality
   c. Access to decision-makers
   d. Keeping a secret

6. Counterfeit detection pens are used to detect:
   a. Wood-based paper
   b. Rag-based paper
   c. Hemp-based paper
   d. Inferior ink

7. Which of the following is *not* part of the fraud triangle?
   a. Rationalization
   b. Concealment
   c. Opportunity
   d. Pressure

8. Fraud is a _____ crime.

    a. Blue-collar

    b. White-collar

    c. Property

    d. Violent

9. The fraud triangle theory was developed by:

    a. Gabriel Tarde

    b. Edwin Sutherland

    c. Ronald Akers

    d. Donald Cressey

10. Which fraud scheme involves stealing payments from one customer and covering the theft with payments stolen from other customers?

    a. Skimming

    b. Lapping

    c. Billing fraud

    d. Graft

11. CryptoLocker is an example of:

    a. Phishing

    b. Ransomware

    c. Spoofing

    d. Money laundering

12. Which of the following is *not* a type of corruption?

    a. Conflict of interest

    b. Bribery

    c. Economic extortion

    d. Asset misappropriation

13. Which of the following is *not* an example of expense reimbursement fraud?

    a. Altering receipts

    b. Splitting expenses

    c. Laundering expenses

    d. Depositing refunds

14. Which type of cyberattack is used to try to take down a government website?

    a. Denial of service

    b. Phishing

    c. Ransomware

    d. Data breach

15. In a(n) _____, a criminal "floods" a network or website with large amounts of information or requests for access.

    a. Larceny scheme

    b. Denial of service attack

    c. Abuse of discretion

    d. Identity theft

16. Which type of asset misappropriation involves stealing cash before it is recorded in the accounting system?

    a. Theft of cash

    b. Lapping

    c. Skimming

    d. Billing scheme

17. Which of the following is *not* a common way to steal data from a computer?

    a. Malware on charging stations

    b. Social networking

    c. Vishing

    d. Hacking

18. The failure to report tips, or to underreport tips, is a form of:

    a. Tax fraud

    b. Payroll fraud

    c. Asset misappropriation

    d. Corruption

19. Which of the following types of payroll frauds uses fictitious employees?

    a. Slow work for overtime

    b. Vacation abuse

    c. Ghost employees

    d. Falsification of hours worked

20. Which of the following accounts receivable frauds involves management misstating the accounts receivable balance to lenders?

    a. Factoring fraud

    b. Payment diversion

    c. Skimming

    d. Check swap

¶ 10,400 Answer Sheets

¶ 10,401 Top Accounting and Auditing Issues for 2021 CPE Course: MODULE 1

Go to **cchcpelink.com/printcpe** to complete your Final Exam online for instant results.

A $90.00 processing fee will be charged for each user submitting Module 1 to **cchcpelink.com/printcpe** online for grading.

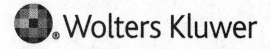

Wolters Kluwer

Module 1: Answer Sheet

Please answer the questions by indicating the appropriate letter next to the corresponding number.

1. _____   10. _____   19. _____

2. _____   11. _____   20. _____

3. _____   12. _____

4. _____   13. _____

5. _____   14. _____

6. _____   15. _____

7. _____   16. _____

8. _____   17. _____

9. _____   18. _____

Please complete the Evaluation Form (located after the Module 3 Answer Sheet). Thank you.

¶ 10,402 Top Accounting and Auditing Issues for 2021 CPE Course: MODULE 2

Go to **cchcpelink.com/printcpe** to complete your Final Exam online for instant results.

A $154.00 processing fee will be charged for each user submitting Module 2 to **cchcpelink.com/printcpe** for online grading.

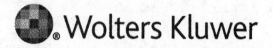

Module 2: Answer Sheet

Please answer the questions by indicating the appropriate letter next to the corresponding number.

1. ___	11. ___	21. ___	31. ___
2. ___	12. ___	22. ___	32. ___
3. ___	13. ___	23. ___	33. ___
4. ___	14. ___	24. ___	34. ___
5. ___	15. ___	25. ___	35. ___
6. ___	16. ___	26. ___	36. ___
7. ___	17. ___	27. ___	37. ___
8. ___	18. ___	28. ___	38. ___
9. ___	19. ___	29. ___	39. ___
10. ___	20. ___	30. ___	40. ___

Please complete the Evaluation Form (located after the Module 3 Answer Sheet). Thank you.

¶ 10,403 Top Accounting and Auditing Issues for 2021 CPE Course: MODULE 3

Go to **cchcpelink.com/printcpe** to complete your Final Exam online for instant results.

A $90.00 processing fee will be charged for each user submitting Module 3 to **cchcpe-link.com/printcpe** for online grading.

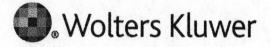

Module 3: Answer Sheet

Please answer the questions by indicating the appropriate letter next to the corresponding number.

1. _____   11. _____

2. _____   12. _____

3. _____   13. _____

4. _____   14. _____

5. _____   15. _____

6. _____   16. _____

7. _____   17. _____

8. _____   18. _____

9. _____   19. _____

10. _____   20. _____

Please complete the Evaluation Form (located after the Module 3 Answer Sheet). Thank you.

¶ 10,500 Top Accounting and Auditing Issues for 2021 CPE Course: Evaluation Form
(10024493-0008)

Please take a few moments to fill out and submit this evaluation to Wolters Kluwer so that we can better provide you with the type of self-study programs you want and need. Thank you.

About This Program

1. Please circle the number that best reflects the extent of your agreement with the following statements:

		Strongly Agree				Strongly Disagree
a.	The Course objectives were met.	5	4	3	2	1
b.	This Course was comprehensive and organized.	5	4	3	2	1
c.	The content was current and technically accurate.	5	4	3	2	1
d.	This Course content was relevant and contributed to achievement of the learning objectives.	5	4	3	2	1
e.	The prerequisite requirements were appropriate.	5	4	3	2	1
f.	This Course was a valuable learning experience.	5	4	3	2	1
g.	The Course completion time was appropriate.	5	4	3	2	1

2. What do you consider to be the strong points of this Course?

3. What improvements can we make to this Course?

THANK YOU FOR TAKING THE TIME TO COMPLETE THIS SURVEY!